The Moore Family

of

Susan Moore, Alabama

C. Marie Currey Jackson

Max Pate

Blount County, Alabama
2012

The Moore Family of Susan Moore, Alabama

Fifth Estate

2795 County Hwy 57

Blountsville, AL 35031

First Edition

Cover Designed by An Quigley

Printed on acid-free paper

Library of Congress Control No: 2012949303

ISBN: 9781936533299

Fifth Estate, 2012

ABOUT THE AUTHORS:

Marie Currey Jackson and Max Pate are graduates of Susan Moore High School and were reared in Clarence, Alabama. Both have a long standing interest in family history and genealogy. This was a joint project spanning more than year of time. Max was the main photographer of current pictures and monuments with assistance from his son Dave. He continuously proofread the copy being prepared by Marie, with the assistance of her husband, Jerry. The stories contributed were compiled and edited by both Max and Marie. Growing up together in the community of Clarence/Susan Moore, and being "first cousins, once removed" we never imagined that we would later undertake this writing!

Marie and her husband, Jerry currently live in Susan Moore on part of the original Moore Farm, about a mile from where she was reared. Marie received her BS and MS degrees from Jacksonville State University, Jacksonville, Alabama and her doctoral degree from the University of Alabama. Her doctoral degree is in Counselor Education. She was also a Licensed Professional Counselor having worked as an outpatient therapist for approximately three years. She taught at Douglas High School in Marshall County, Alabama, and was the high school counselor there until receiving her doctoral degree. Her university teaching included positions at Jacksonville State University, University of Alabama, Gadsden Center, Valdosta State University and University of West Georgia where she taught counselor education and was involved in research and writing. She is married to Jerry R. Jackson and they have three sons, and six grandchildren. Now, she is a retired professor who has invested most of her retirement years in genealogy and writing. She enjoys playing the piano, writing poetry, and traveling, especially to the beach.

Max and his wife Betty live in Pinson, Alabama and Max is a graduate of Susan Moore High School. Growing up in the community of Susan Moore among the Moore family descendants and being related to some of the Moore family members gave him a special interest in family history and genealogy. He is now retired from Thompson Tractor Company after a lifetime career with that company. He is married to Betty Baker Pate and they have two sons, and one grandson. Max is a lover of golf as well as genealogy. He enjoys tending his flowers and yard. His parents were Rex and Ruth Pate who were known for growing and developing daylilies. Max contributes to 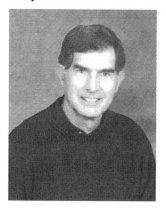 this community in a variety of ways. He has voluntarily repaired broken cemetery markers and along with others, mowed, and cleaned off the Lamb Cemetery. He is a participating member of the Blount County Memorial Museum and enjoys exploring the history of Blount County.

ACKNOWLEDGEMENTS

Without the assistance of others this writing would never have been completed. We have so many to recognize and thank for their assistance, encouragement and contributions. I first want to thank my husband, Jerry R. Jackson for his diligent work in formatting the pictures for this book and proofreading and correcting many things throughout the duration of this writing. He has been most patient and supportive. We have had willing support from those in the community and from other areas. Relatives and friends throughout the area were helpful as we asked questions and were attempting to locate pictures and stories to make the history of the Moore Family and this community as complete as possible. No book of this sort can be written without some error, but we have made numerous attempts to provide accurate information.

A list of contributors Max and I wish to specifically acknowledge follows:

Lilma Yancey Adams; Glynn and Bobbie Debtor; Robert Duran Sloman; Vernell Elrod; Robbie Bryan; Peggy Bryan Jenkins; Dave Pate; Kay Adams Smallwood; Johnny Adams; Bill Haynes; Bob Moore; Mike Moore; Mary Holland Kerney; Betty Jo Ashley; Odis Huffstutler; Edna Bryan; Lillie Mae Brown; Janice Tidwell White; and Bill Smallwood.

We also want to thank Amy Rhudy, and the Blount County Memorial Museum for encouragement and assistance to write, compile and publish this book.

My grandfather, C. Claude Moore (1882 – 1962) was the benefactor of numerous pictures used within this book. He deserves so much honor and respect for the encouragement he gave me throughout my childhood years and I personally want to recognize him for having given me the pictures, the oral and written history, as well as being the role model that he was in my life and the lives of others.

Contents

Dr. David S. Moore Sr. and Dr. David S. Moore Jr.

Introduction

Susan Moore, Alabama! How did this small community and local school get its name? I recall many years ago being asked where I lived and I responded, proudly, "Susan Moore". The person who asked me had a quizzical look on his face and said, "No, what is the name of the PLACE where you live? Not your name..." Well, I soon learned that I had to be careful about telling people where I lived lest they think it was my name! I did grow up knowing the stories of Susan Moore, the school; Clarence, the place; and Susan Moore, the person. My grandfather, Professor C. Claude Moore, lived in our home from 1950 when my grandmother died until his death in 1962. Many stories were shared around the fireplace in the evenings; those type experiences rarely are a part of family life today as it was in those days. I learned a lot from my Grandfather Moore and my mother, Ivaleen Moore Currey, about the Moore families and the history of this community. We are preparing this book to share our memories, research, and collection of historical and current photographs relative to the pioneer family, specifically, Robert M. Moore and his descendants. Many family and community members have contributed to this work. We wish to clearly and accurately answer questions about the history of our town.

Where and when did this town of Susan Moore really begin? In 1850, the United States Federal Census shows people living in the section of Blount County that later became the Susan Moore/Clarence area. Most living here at that time, if not all, were farmers. Some of the family names are familiar, such as Bynum, Scruggs, and Thompsons. However, by 1860, in addition to the farmers, there were merchants, blacksmiths, wagon makers, physicians and millers.

The number of residences in Blount County appeared to have doubled between 1850 and 1860. A community was beginning to come together. The civil war was on the horizon and there was much political and social unrest. People were moving westward, seeking fertile soil for farming, and a better life.

As we explore the origin of the community of Clarence (later named Susan Moore) we will take a look at the family and historical background and contributions of the Robert M. Moore family who settled in the Eastern section of Blount County, Alabama. Who was Robert M. Moore and what brought him here to Blount County? Where did he live before he came here?

Robert M. Moore was the son of Zachariah Moore and Mary Still Moore of Walton County, Georgia. Mary Still was the daughter of Benjamin Still and Mary Jane Martin Still. Other names in her direct line other than Still are Jolly, Brockington, Dunn, and Taylor. Mary's family came to Georgia from Edgefield District of South Carolina. Zachariah's parents also were reported in the census to have been born in South Carolina. Zachariah and Mary married the 25th of December 1823. They gave birth to 10 children, (5 girls and 5 boys). A brief overview of these children introduces the Moore family background. The eldest child was a girl, Nancy Sidney Moore Morgan, who married near the time of her father's death. She and her husband, William L. Billy Morgan relocated to Ellis, Texas and lived the remainder of their lives in that location. The second child was Robert M., who left Walton County, Georgia about the same time as his sister, Nancy. He and his family came to Blount County, Alabama. The third child, Elizabeth "Betsy" Moore Watson lived with her husband, Elisha Bennett Watson near Rossville, Georgia in 1870. She died in 1885 and is buried in Shiloh Primitive Baptist Cemetery in Walton County, Georgia. Her husband remarried and he and his second wife moved to Navarro, Texas and lived out their lives there. All of Betsy and Elisha Bennett Watson's children had moved to Texas prior to his second marriage and relocation. Elisha Bennett Watson was a brother to Robert M Moore's wife, Nancy J. Watson.

The fourth child of Zachariah, Sallie M. only lived for three years. The next five children remained in Walton County Georgia for the duration of their lives with the exception that the youngest child, Thomas relocated to Ellis, Texas after his first wife's death and lived there until his death in 1927. Zachariah's wife, Mary lived 20 years longer than her husband. Zachariah and Mary Still Moore are buried in the Moore Cemetery near Double Springs Baptist Church in Walton County, Georgia.

Moore Cemetery in Walton County, Georgia

Burial site of Zachariah Moore and Mary Still Moore near Double Springs Baptist Church.

Moore Monument in Moore Cemetery in Walton County, Georgia

It is interesting to note that the two eldest children left Walton County while their mother was still living, leaving her behind after their father's death which had occurred December 18, 1860. For some unknown reason, Zachariah cannot be found in the census of 1860 just prior to his death. Zachariah's wife, Mary was recorded in the 1860 census as the head of the family living on her own farm. She was listed as a farmer at the age of 57. Living with her at that time was her son David Martin Moore, age 19, a daughter, Sarah, age 23, and the youngest son, Thomas, age 15. Martha was 3 years younger than Sarah, unmarried as far as we know; but is not shown living with any of the family at the time of the 1860 census.

By 1870, Martha and Sarah Ann are living with their mother, Mary Still Moore. Mary's residence was near several of her Still family members. She was shown as the owner of her farm and only one other family listed on the census page was shown to own their farm. By 1880, Mary was living with her daughter and son-in-law, Betsy and Elisha B. Watson. Mary was reported to be widowed and 76 years old at that time. Her daughter Martha is still unmarried at age 38 and living with the Watson's also. There are many unanswered questions about Zachariah and Mary Still Moore during these troubled times. Another interesting fact about the Zachariah Moore family is that four of the sons, William Young Moore, Benjamin Still Moore, David Martin Moore and Thomas Jefferson Moore all served in the Civil War in Co. D, 2nd Regiment, GA Volunteer Cavalry from 1861-1864 and all returned home alive. As we begin to focus on the pioneer family of Moore's, (Robert M. Moore) who came to Blount County, we can begin to understand the historical time frame and the setting as certainly that of the Civil War era. What we know is that Zachariah had died December 18, 1860 and his eldest children were moving out of Georgia while four of the younger sons had joined to fight in the civil war. Mary was living with two of her children and running the family farm. Perhaps those that were leaving Georgia were seeking safety and a better life for their families.

Chapter 1

Robert M. Moore Pioneer Blount Countian

Sometime, after 1860, and prior to 1865, Robert Marian Moore came to North Alabama. He found alluring hills and rich farm land on the southern tip of Sand Mountain in the eastern portion of Blount County. He returned to Walton County and persuaded his wife, Nancy Jane Watson Moore, and their children to return with him to Blount County to build a home and a new life. Legend has it that they came in a covered wagon to the section of land that Robert had entered on his first trip. The story has been told that Robert came on that first trip in an oxcart.

This picture of an oxcart and a few Moore family men is from the C. Claude Moore Family collection of photographs now in the possession of his granddaughter, Marie Currey Jackson. Could this have been the oxcart that Robert M. Moore used on his way to Blount County? It may have been the actual oxcart used by Robert on his first trip, but we do not know that for sure.

The children of Robert M. Moore and Nancy Jane Watson Moore were:

1.	William T. Moore	B. Dec 10 1847	D. About 1865
2.	Zachariah E. Moore	B. Feb 20 1849	D. Jul 21 1924
3.	Robert Bennett Moore	B. Oct 16 1850	D. Sep 3 1901
4.	David Sanders Moore	B. Mar 19 1852	D. Dec 9 1932
5.	Benjamin Martin Moore	B. Mar 24 1854	D. Feb25 1943
6.	John Morgan Moore	B. Sep 17 1855	D. Aug 1 1935
7.	James Hamilton Moore	B. Mar 08 1858	D. Mar 27 1939
8.	Daniel Marion Moore	B. Aug 13 1859	D. Sep 7 1942
9.	Nancy Elizabeth Moore	B. Aug 13 1861	D. Jun 22 1892
10.	Mary Emma Moore	B. Aug 08 1864	D. Nov 12 1912

Often, very little is said about the wives and mothers of the early pioneers when a family story is written. Yet, not enough can be said about a mother of 10 children who reared them to adulthood with many successes along the way. She also experienced many traumatic events and hardships in her family. She was the daughter of Elisha Watson and Christina Morgan. The granddaughter of John and Ann Watson, she outlived her husband by more than 30 years. She was laid to rest by the side of Robert M. Moore at Salem Primitive Baptist Cemetery just off Highway 278 W of Snead, AL near Brooksville. She died in November 24, 1910.

Robert M. Moore and Nancy J. Watson's monument in Salem Cemetery

Sleep Father and take thy rest   Having served her generation
God called thee home –   She now sweetly rests
He thought it best

The Robert M. Moore Family
Back Row: John M. Moore, Benjamin Martin Moore, James Hamilton Moore, Zachariah
E. Moore, Robert Bennett Moore. Front Row: David Sanders Moore, Daniel Marion
Moore, Nancy J. Watson Moore, Nancy A. E. Moore, Emma Moore

William T. Moore was the first son of Robert M. Moore and Nancy J. Watson Moore. He was born 10 December 1847 in Walton County, Georgia. According to family records, William had died near the end of the Civil War around the time Robert came to Blount County. There are some conflicting stories about William's death. Some report that he was in school in Nashville, Tennessee and died as a result of an accident. It is reported by at least one researcher that he died in the Civil War. We have no record of a marriage for William T. Moore and no known place of burial.

Moore Brothers – the longest surviving children of Robert M. and Nancy Moore, David Sanders, Benjamin Martin, John Morgan, James Hamilton, and Daniel Marion

Chapter 2
The Second Son of Robert M. Moore

Zachariah E. Moore, the second child was named for his Grandfather Zachariah Moore. Some family researchers say that the first Zachariah's middle name began with a C. while the grandson was Zachariah Elisha Moore. Zachariah E. was born in Walton County on Feb 20 1849, married Josephine Nunnley of Georgia in 1870 in Walton County, Georgia. Zack and Josie (as they were called) had four children born to them. The only one to live to adulthood was Ida Vesta Moore who married Frank Muse. He was reared in Carrollton, GA. Frank came to Alabama and was a farm laborer for Zachariah, later marrying Zachariah's daughter, Ida. This sounds like the classic love story of the farm hand marrying the farmer's daughter! Ida and Frank lived a long life together and had no children. Frank served the local community as a policeman and in later years worked in Gadsden, Alabama in law enforcement. Both, Frank and Ida are interred at Wynnville Cemetery (at the intersection of County Road 34 and Co. Rd 36) in the first "above ground" mausoleum in the cemetery.

Zack and Josie's other children were Nancy Caroline, who only lived 11 years; James T.

Moore who only lived two years; and a third child, Inzer Alexander Moore, who lived to be 17 years of age. Zach, Josie, and all the children are buried in Wynnville Cemetery. Zach died July 21, 1924.

To illustrate life in the Clarence community and in the Zack Moore family, in the 1920s, the following is an excerpt that first appeared in THE SOUTHERN DEMOCRAT in 1921. It was written by Jesse Burns.

Great Day at Uncle Zack Moore's

January 1, 1921 was a great day for Uncle Zack and Aunt Josie Moore, when they called together their friends and relatives to enjoy with them and witness an occasion that but few ever witness—their golden wedding anniversary

You will notice that we addressed Mr. Moore as "Uncle Zack". He is called Uncle Zack by everyone. He is honored and respected by everybody who knows him.

They were married January 1, 1871 at 9:30 a.m. near Lawrenceville, Georgia. They remained there until the 8 day of January. In the afternoon of that day they started on their honeymoon—not in a flying machine, automobile, or in a Pullman, but in a two-horse tar poll wagon with bow frame and sheet. This trip was made to Blount County, Alabama, their future home.

They were accompanied by his brothers, Dr. David S. Moore and the late R. B. Moore. They spent the first night in Lawrenceville. On the 9th day they started on their long journey. That night was spent with his aunt, Mrs. Betsie Watson, near Rossville, Georgia. Next day they continued their journey with the same degree of happiness. On the night of the 10th they camped a little east of Statesboro, Georgia. This being a rainy night, you can imagine the pleasure they enjoyed.

The 11th was a cold windy day, and that night was spent around a campfire at Silver Creek, five miles south of Rome, Georgia. The 12th was somewhat more pleasant, which they enjoyed very much; and that night they camped near Centre, Alabama. The 13 was another rainy day, and as the evening shadows began to fall they went into camp on the top of Sand Mountain, this side of Attalla.

Early next morning they started on the last lap of their journey. Noon of this day, the 14 of January, found them at the home of the late John H. Campbell (W. J. Kerr now owns the place) who had prepared them a sumptuous infair dinner, which was served with the characteristic southern hospitality of that day. One of the luxuries served was apple brandy so old that it would rope.

In the afternoon they proceeded on their journey. Late in the afternoon they reached his father's which brought them to the end of the journey. They lived in the house with his father until laying-by time; they bought a farm near Ebenezer Church and lived there until 1880. In 1880 they entered 160 acres of land one mile north of their first home. They had to cut out a road to their present home and started anew in the woods—not a foot of cleared land.

Uncle Jim Lamb was the only person present who was living here fifty years ago. The following relatives were present: Ida Muse, B. M. Moore and wife, J. M. Moore and wife, J. R. Moore and wife, Dr. D. S. Moore and wife, Robert Moore and family, Jesse M. Burns and family, and Claude Moore. Friends present were I. C. Tidwell and wife, Orion Wright, Mrs. Anna Wright, James S. Lamb and wife, Thomas J. Chadwick, Troy Elrod, Duet Wright and wife, Euel Wright, Mrs. Lamar Engle and Children, Mrs. Diller Walker and child, Mrs. Parolee Robertson and children, Mrs. Ross Harris and Mrs. Hatley. The total number for dinner was forty-three.

Once again we look back to 1870, to their first wedding. Then twenty-five years elapsed for their silver wedding. Now fifty years are in history and Uncle Zack and Aunt Josie are still hale and hearty to enjoy this Golden Wedding.

(Obtained from Susan Moore 1865-1989. Reunion Committee)

Chapter 3
The Third Son of Robert M. Moore

Robert Bennett Moore. Bennett was born Oct 16, 1850 and died September 3, 1901. His wife was Sarah Elizabeth Hicks (1853-1931). The Robert Bennett Moore home place was located on the road given as the Oneonta to High Mound Road. Bennett was a farmer and owned property along and east of present day State Road Highway 75. Robert Bennett Moore's wife was the daughter of James Washington Hicks and Frances Lewton Hicks. James Washington Hicks was a Civil War Veteran. His Civil War Monument located in Lamb Cemetery states that he was in the 15th Alabama Infantry. Sarah Elizabeth's parents, both are buried in the Lamb Cemetery on the C. Claude Moore and Ada Lamb Moore home place on Highway 75 just north of the Susan Moore Town Hall. Their graves are among the few remaining ones with markers. Robert Bennett Moore and his wife, Sarah Elizabeth Hicks Moore were buried in Mt. Moriah Cemetery.

Bennett and Elizabeth Moore were the parents of the first principal of Susan Moore High School, William Augustus "Gus" Moore. In addition to Gus, Robert Bennett Moore had two daughters, one was Villulia, who married Arthur Phillips and the third child was Vanda Mae Moore who never married and died at the age of 21.

William A. "Gus" Moore

William Augustus (Gus) Moore was born April 29, 1875 at Clarence, Alabama. He attended Blount College at Blountsville, Alabama and received his B.S. from Howard College, now Samford University, in Birmingham on August 20, 1932. He was married to Tera Coats Moore on November 3, 1897. They lived in a two story colonial type home that stood on the east side of Highway 75 at the intersection of Ridgeway Drive and State Rd 75 about a mile north of the Susan Moore Town Hall

William Augustus "Gus" Moore's Home

Gus and Terah had a daughter to die in infancy in 1889. Etoile Moore, their second

daughter was born 23 Oct 1901. She married Orris Martin and together they had one child, William Moore Martin, commonly, called Billy. Billy Moore Martin was born 18 Feb 1929 and died 1 Nov 2001. Donald Peter Martin and James David Martin were sons of Billy Moore Martin and great grandsons of Gus Moore.

A good old fashion "barn raising" for Gus Moore by community members.

Gus Moore's barn after completion

Professor Gus Moore was active across Blount County in service organizations. He was a charter member of the Oneonta Civitan Club and served as President 1937-38. He was of the Primitive Baptist belief as were many of the Moore family members. His special interests were education in all its aspects; home; meeting and talking with people, young and old.

In addition to his interest in education, Professor Moore was also a civic minded man and served on the Blount County Board of Welfare from his original appointment in 1935 through 1952. He served as Chairman of the Welfare Board the entire time he was a member except the first three months. He began his teaching career at age 18 and it has been told that he set his goal at 50 years; however, he exceeded his goal. After leaving Susan Moore in 1942 because of his health, he later taught at Blount County High School in Oneonta (The Heritage of Blount County, 1972). He died April 14, 1956 and is buried in Mt. Moriah Cemetery, Blount County near Fridays Crossing just east of Highway 75

Gus and Tera Moore

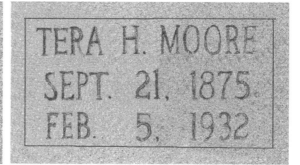

Villulia A. Moore, (1879-1924) daughter of Robert Bennett Moore, married Arthur Phillips. Eight children were born to Villulia and Arthur Phillips, beginning with Coy and Roy followed by two daughters, Rubye, who married Raymond Bayliss and Pearl, who married Bill Gullege. A third son, Arthur Phillips, Jr. married Lena Hudson. Arthur and Lena had two daughters, Virginia Lee, and Jean. Virginia married Emmett Doyle. Jean married Max Blackmon. Both Virginia and Jean graduated from Susan Moore High, were cheerleaders and class beauties during their years there. Three more children were born to Villulia and Arthur, Sr., a son Aubrey who married Cecelia Johnston; a daughter, Opal who married Bill Lanier. The youngest child, born in 1919 was Grady W Phillips who became a medical doctor. As a grandson of Robert Bennett Moore, his interesting life history taken from his obituary deserves repeating here:

> *Phillips, M.D., Grady W.* Grady was born in Gadsden, Alabama, May 16, 1919 and died of natural causes in Dallas, Texas, July 20, 2008. He is survived by a daughter, Fran Phillips; granddaughter, Currin Berdine; former son-in-law, Scott Berdine; son, Grady W. Phillips, Jr., daughter-in-law Marilyn Phillips; and grandchildren, Bill and Elizabeth Phillips. Two events shaped his life - the Great Depression and the death of his mother from cancer. From the former he learned to save everything. From the latter, he dedicated his life to medicine. He graduated from the University of Alabama and Emory Medical School where he married Doris Cockerham, who was also in medical school. He completed post doctorate work at St. Agnes in Baltimore, the University of Alabama, and the University of Chicago where he specialized in Obstetrics and Gynecology and pivotal cancer research. Grady was a Captain in the 8th Army. He served at the 34th Station Hospital in Rome, Italy where he provided medical care to the Embassy. He also operated Clinical Bonanome, near the Vatican. He delivered some 100 babies to the American colony before delivering his own daughter, Fran. He also served at Walter Reed in Washington, D.C. He delivered a child to Shirley Temple Black. He completed his military obligation in rural Mississippi. Grady moved to Illinois in the late 1950s to work at Barnes Hospital, St. Louis and operated a clinic in Belleville. In 1970 he was shot and partially paralyzed. He used his experiences as an asset and served on the Nursing Home Advisory Council of Illinois and at the VFW. He moved to Dallas in 1994 and became active in Park Cities Baptist Church. His family will miss his smile, stories and jokes and remember him as a strong Christian and a talented doctor. (Taken in part from the Roots Web List serve).

Villulia Armelia Moore Phillips

Blount College Students

J. D. Patton - 1900   **(Right) Claude Moore**   **Classmates**

Chapter 4

The Fourth Son of Robert M. Moore

Dr. David S. Moore Sr.

Dr. David Sanders Moore, Sr. and Family

Front: Fannie Moore Dean

1st Row: T. Clarence Moore and wife Clint Moore, Susan Moore, Dr. David S. Moore

2nd Row: Dr. Joseph G. Moore, Annie Pettus Moore,

Dr. David S. Moore Jr., Mary Pearl Moore Dean, Eugene Dean

Who is the real Susan Moore? A large number of females among the descendants of the Robert M. Moore family have been named Susan Moore. So, it is a valid question for someone to question as to which Susan Moore was the one for whom the school and this town was named. In order to answer that question among others, we need to review the next child of Robert M. Moore, **David Sanders Moore, Sr.**, who received his medical degree from Atlanta Medical College in Georgia about 1873. He and his wife, Susan A. Nunnalley married the 25th of March, 1875. They built a home near the heart of the community where Robert M. Moore had settled.

The first child, born in 1876, of Dr. David and Susan Moore was Taliaferro Clarence Moore. As a child, Clarence played around the area as people visited the office and drug store. By 1883, Dr. David Moore named the community surrounding his home Clarence to honor his first borne son, Talliferro Clarence. Clarence was seven years old at that time. By 1890, the Post Office for the community of Clarence was established and opened in the Brick building that housed Dr. Davy's office. The Clarence Post Office closed in 1907 (Jim Forte's United States Postal history).

Susan Alexandria Nunnalley Moore, the wife of Dr. David S. Moore, Sr. eventually became the "Susan Moore" for whom the school was named. The home of Susan Moore and Dr. David S. Moore Sr. was built soon after their marriage and was located near the site of the Moore Mansion.

Home of David S. and Susan Moore
The original picture is located in "The Cabbage Patch Museum" at Robbie Bryan's home

Two of the younger sons had followed in their father's footsteps so to speak and also became medical doctors, Dr. David S. Moore, Jr. and Dr. Joseph Grover Moore referred to by many as Dr. D. and Dr. Joe. These men built a large antebellum type home in the center of Clarence on their farm. The house stood where Wilburn and Joree Adams built their home which is now the residence of Wilburn and Joree's daughter, Kay Adams Smallwood. The Moore mansion was an impressive structure, in my memory, with a staircase spiraling down into a foyer with a large chandelier. For its time and place it was unique. To a young girl such as me, it was like something out of a movie.

The home of Dr. D. S. Moore, Jr., and Dr. Joe G. Moore, in Clarence, Alabama

Since Dr. Dee and Dr. Joe resided in Birmingham during the work week, they only traveled to Clarence on the weekends. Ellis Dean and his wife Mildred Bradford Dean were living in the home at the time the house was lost to a fire in the 1950s. Ellis was the grandson of Dr. David S. Moore, and the son of Eugene O. Dean and Pearl Moore Dean. Pearl was a sister to the medical doctors. Mildred, Ellis' wife, was a first grade teacher at Susan Moore. The loss of the home was a sad time in Clarence. The home had been a landmark for the community, sitting just east of Susan Moore High School.

Dr. Dee and Dr. Joe are remembered for having primarily financed the building of Susan Moore High School and in return only asking that the school be named in honor of their mother, Susan. For many years, the community remained Clarence, and the school was Susan Moore High School. Both names, Clarence and Susan Moore are on some maps today identifying locations along Susan Moore road and both, are in recognition of family members of Dr. David S. Moore, Sr. Today, the town is officially, Susan Moore, having been incorporated in 1982. So, let's take a closer look at those people for whom the community, the town and the school are named. Let's begin with the namesake of Clarence community, Talliferro Clarence Moore.

So, Who in the World was Clarence?

Telaferro Clarence Moore
29 April 1876
8 January 1923

The story of the naming of Susan Moore School is more widely known than the naming of Clarence community. Some people today are not even aware that this town was once named Clarence. Who exactly was the person for whom Clarence was named? Not too many people living today in 2012 know much about him. *Taliaferro Clarence Moore* was born April 29, 1876 and died January 8, 1923. He was the son of **Dr. David Sanders Moore** and his wife Susan. Clarence married in 1899 to Clinton "Clint" Montgomery, the daughter of Clinton and Eliza Barcliff Montgomery of Blountsville. She was also a relative of Judge J. E. Blackwood of Oneonta. Clarence was the grandson of Robert and Nancy Watson Moore and of Jackson and Nancy Bonds Nunnalley, all of Georgia. Famous people in his background were the renowned Tom Watson of Georgia, and from his mother's family, the Charley Smith and the Van Bibbers who were the founders of Baltimore. Even though born with a fine heritage, Clarence personally accomplished much on his own in his 47 years of life. Quoting from a History of Alabama and Dictionary of Alabama Biography, Vol. IV, 1921 located in the state archives, "he attended schools in Clarence, 1882-1890; entered Blount College, Blountsville, where he was graduated A. B. and M. Acct; and was graduated from the University of Alabama in 1903 receiving the degrees of B.S. and M.S in the same year." A register of the University of Alabama students (1901) listed him as having been a teacher at Blount College in 1896-97, and Vice President and Instructor at Central Agricultural College at that time. The 1902 University of Alabama catalog of students listed his degrees as being in Geology, Chemistry, and Astronomy and his course as Schools. His Master's Thesis topic is particularly interesting. It was "Geological Relations of the Deposits of Hematite and Limonite in the Birmingham District of Alabama". In 1902, Clarence was studying about the deposits containing various iron ore compositions probably on Red Mountain. His story does not end here. Professor T.C. Moore had begun teaching school at the age of 13 with a first grade certificate and taught continuously from that early age. In addition to teaching in the rural Blount county schools, he served as English Professor for four years in the 9th District Agricultural School at Blountsville; as Principal for two years in the Talladega City High School; President for three years of the 4th District Agricultural School at Sylacauga (present day Sylacauga High School); and as the Principal of Blount County High School in Oneonta, Alabama for a number of years. According to his obituary from the Southern Democrat (January 11, 1923, Number 16) Clarence was the first principal of the Blount County High School (Oneonta) and served there from 1911 to 1918 and "made it the best high school in the state during his administration". At the time of his death, he was employed by the Jefferson County Board of Education and, served as the principal of the school near where his funeral was held, ACIPCO, the community of American Cast Iron and Pipe Company. The students were dismissed from school and attended his funeral at the ACIPCO Methodist Church as a group in honor of their former principal. He was highly involved in the Methodist Church, serving in many capacities. He was a Mason, a member of the Zamora Temple and Cyrene Commandery. Perhaps, he had been a member of Clarence Masonic Lodge 708, once located in the heart of Clarence Community and that lodge is now in the year 2012 located in Snead, Alabama approximately 3 miles north of Susan Moore Town Hall. Needless to say, Taliaferro Clarence Moore was an educated and honored man. One such honor was membership in Kappa Sigma College Fraternity. According to his obituary, he had also graduated from Columbia College in New York, most likely completing his doctorate in education there. He and his wife, Clint are buried in Elmwood Cemetery, Jefferson County, Alabama.

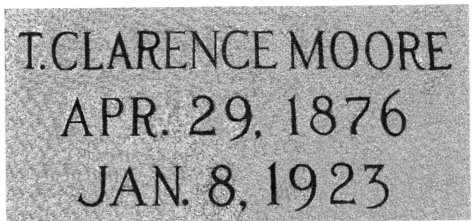

PROF. T. C. MOORE AND WIFE BURIED IN ELMWOOD CEMETERY IN BIRMINGHAM, ALABAMA

Funeral services will be held for Professor Moore at 11 o'clock Wednesday morning from the Acipco Methodist church, with Dr. Lester of Oneonta and Rev. J. S. Blackburn of the Acipco church in charge. Students of the school will attend in a body, the institution being closed all day Wednesday as a mark of respect to the former principal, who died Monday afternoon at a Birmingham hospital. Burial will be in Elmwood Cemetery. Pallbearers will be: W. E. Dickson, Prof. R. A. Duvall, Prof. R. V. Allgood, Prof. R. C. Johnson, Dr. Charles A. Brown and H. G. Dyer.

Note: Some places the reader may see T. Clarence Moore's first name reported to be Tolaver. The references that these writers located documenting his name as Taliferro are a biography found in the Alabama State Archives, his University of Alabama degree listing, and a catalog of students at the University of Alabama as well as a U.S. passport to England.

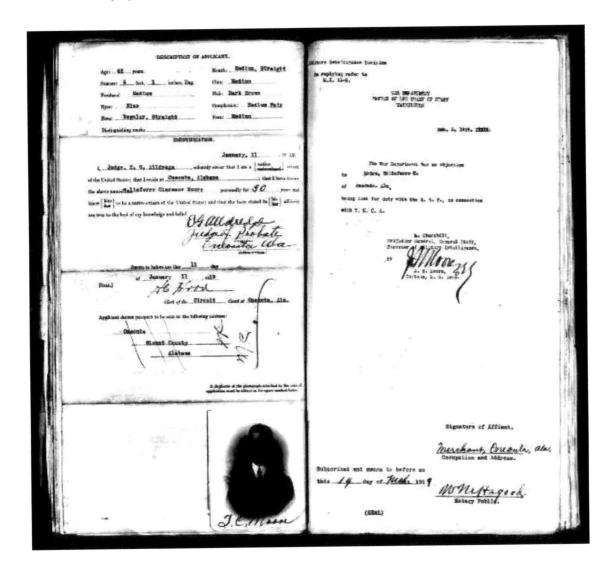

Passports provide interesting information. According to this document, Clarence's first name was Taliaferro. He was 42 years of age in 1919, had blue eyes and brown hair with a medium complexion. He was 6 feet and 1 inch tall. Judge E. G. Alldredge, the Judge of Probate in Oneonta, Alabama provided a sworn statement of identification that he had known Taliaferro Clarence Moore personally for 30 years and knew him to be a native citizen of the United States and that the facts in his affidavit were true....Jan 1l, 1919 Witnessed by C. Hood, Circuit Clerk of Oneonta, Alabama.

The second child of David S. and Susan was *Robert Jackson Moore*, the name Robert, obviously was selected because it was the given name of his Grandfather Moore and the name Jackson was the given name of his Grandfather Nunnalley. This naming follows the typical naming patterns of the era. I don't know exactly what led Robert J. to Travis, Austin, Texas; but, you may recall that several people from the previous generation in Walton County had relocated to this general area in Texas. His Great Aunt Betsy Moore had married a Watson. Bob, as Robert J. was known, married Eleanor Alma Watson in Texas. She was a distant relative of his Aunt Betsy's husband. Bob was living there with Eleanor and their one year old daughter, Merle, in 1910 according to the Federal Census. At that time, he had been married four years, was living with his father-in-law, William Watson and working as a rate clerk for State Fire Insurance. He continued living in the same area, listed as Travis, Austin, Texas until his death in 1949. He and his family are buried in City Cemetery in Travis, Texas.

Dr. D. S. Moore, Jr. was widely known as a Birmingham surgeon, making his final home in Birmingham, 2830 10TH avenue S. Dr. David S. Moore, Jr. was born on April 11, 1886 in Blount County, Alabama. He was the sixth child of his parents, David S. and Susan Moore. He attended Blount College in Blountsville as a young man. Graduating from the school in Blountsville in 1904 after it became a State Agricultural College. The picture above was made in 1903 when he was a student at Blount College. He received his Medical degree from the University of Alabama in 1908. He traveled to many cities to study surgery at various hospitals. One card was sent to C. Claude Moore in 1916 while he was observing surgery in Philadelphia. The second card was sent while he was visiting the battle grounds of Lexington and Concord.

OLD NORTH BRIDGE. Here took place about noon, April 19th. 1775, the principal engagement in Concord, the British being repulsed and retreating in great disorder. Across the bridge the statue of the "Concord Minute Man"

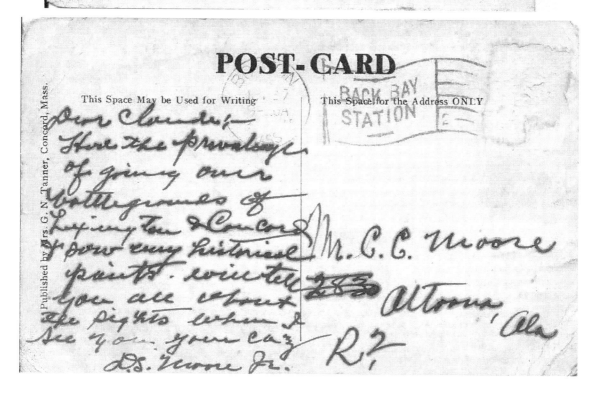

Dr. David S. Moore, Jr. was the president of South Highlands Infirmary, director of surgical services and surgeon-in-chief at Hillman-Jefferson Hospital, and had received numerous honors and recognitions; one of which was the highest honor to be obtained in the medical field, to be made a member of the American Board of Surgery. His obituary printed in the local county newspaper best presents an accounting of his work and life.

Obituary in Thursday, June 12, 1947 "Southern Democrat, "Oneonta, Alabama

DR. MOORE DIES AT BIRMINGHAM HOME

Dr. David Sanders Moore, 61 2830 10th Avenue south (Birmingham), widely known Birmingham surgeon, died early Sunday morning at the residence (June 8, 1947).

Funeral services were held at 4 p.m. Monday at the residence with Dr. Marvin A. Franklin, pastor of Highlands Methodist church, officiating. Burial was in Oak Hill Cemetery (Birmingham).

Dr. Moore who received his M.D. degree from the University of Alabama in 1908 was president of South Highlands Infirmary. He also was director of surgical services and surgeon in chief at Hillman-Jefferson Hospital. He was secretary of the Hospital Service Corporation of Alabama, permanent contributing member of the Shiners Hospital for Crippled Children and member of the Alabama Hospital Association and of the Executive Committee. He was a member of the Jefferson County Medical Society and councilor of the Medical Association of the State of Alabama, member of the American Medical Association, the Birmingham Surgical Society and of Southern Medical Association.

Dr. Moore received the highest honor obtainable in his field when, as a member of the American College of Surgeons, he was made a member of the American Board of Surgery.

He was a member of Highlands Methodist Church, (Birmingham), also held membership in Mountain Brook in Mountain Brook Country Club and was a Mason, a life member of Farrar Lodge #8.

Born in Clarence (Alabama) April 11, 1886, Dr Moore was the son of Dr David Sanders Moore, Sr. and Mrs. Susan Nunnely Moore. He was graduated from the State Secondary Agricultural College, Blountsville, in 1904.

He was married to Miss Annie Pettus of Birmingham November 29, 1910.

In 1925 he became Surgeon-in-Chief at south Highlands Infirmary and was associated in practicing surgery wit Dr. E M. Prince until 1937.

Dr. Moore has always remained a Blount Countian at heart He never refused a person from his home county, medical or surgical treatment because of lack of financial ability. He and his brother, Dr. Joe Moore were always liberal of their time and means for the betterment of their home community and Blount County. It was largely through their efforts that the Susan Moore High School was located at Clarence. (They provided much of the financing and people of the community helped with the labor and hauling. The school was named for their mother.)

Besides his interest in education, Dr. Moore had a life-long interest in farming. He was visiting at his country home only the day before his death. He has spent much time in the last few years at his home in Clarence.

Home of Dr. D. S. Moore Jr. in Birmingham

Photographed 2011 by Max and Dave Pate

Obituary for Dr. David Moore, Jr. from Birmingham News June 10 1947

Final Services Held For Dr. David Moore

Funeral services for Dr. David Sanders Moore, 61, 2830 10th Avenue, South were held yesterday afternoon at the residence. Dr. Moore, widely known Birmingham surgeon, died Sunday morning. Dr. Marvin A. Franklin, pastor of Highlands Methodist Church, conducted the services. Burial was in Oak Hill, Ridout's Brown-Service in charge. Dr. Moore, who received his degree from the University of Alabama, was president of South Highland's Infirmary. He also was director of surgical services and surgeon-in-chief at Hillman-Jefferson Hospital. He was a member of the American Medical Association, the Jefferson County medical Society, the Southern Medical Society, and the Birmingham Surgical Society. Dr. Moore was a member of the American College of Surgeons. He received the highest honor obtainable in his field when he was elected to the American Board of Surgery. He was a member of Highlands Methodist Church, the Mountain Brook Country Club and was a life member of Farrar Lodge No. 8, Masons. Surviving are the widow, the former Miss Annie Pettus, of Birmingham, and two brothers. Dr. Joseph G, Moore, Birmingham, and R. J. Moore, McDade, Tex. (adapted from The Birmingham News, June 10, 1947).

Headstone and Markers for Dr. D. S. Moore, Jr. and his wife Annie Pettus Moore in Oak Hill Cemetery, Birmingham, AL

Dr. Joseph Grover Moore, "Dr. Joe", the seventh child of the elder Dr. Moore and Susan was born March 10, 1888 at Clarence, Alabama. He, like his brother also attended Blount College (State Agricultural School in Blountsville, Alabama) and obtained his medical degree from the University of Alabama in 1911. He traveled in relation to his work in the medical field and sent postcards to relatives back home. One such card is shown here. This card from New Orleans was sent by Dr. Joe when he was on his way to Rosedale, CA.

He married Lucille Catherine Ford of Birmingham, on 20 May 1941. He was a member of the honorary medical fraternity, Theta Kappa Psi, the Jefferson County Medical Society, Medical Association of the State of Alabama, American Medical Association, Southern Medical Association, Birmingham Surgical Society, Charter member of Birmingham Sportsmen's Hunting Club, being particularly fond of hunting; writing poetry, reading, playing different musical instruments and was a great lover of flowers. With his brother, Dr. David Sanders

Moore, Jr., and Dr. Edmond M. Prince he was one-third owner of South Highland Infirmary, being chief surgeon for many years, secretary of this institution in 1925 and vice-president from 1937 until his death on 20 July, 1953 after being in ill health for eight years with a circulatory condition and complications. Burial was in Elmwood Cemetery, Birmingham. He was a member of the Southside Baptist Church and Birmingham Country Club.

Dr. Joseph G. Moore

Dr. Joe received many honors but the greatest of them in his own view as well as his family's view may have been the fact that he was held in great esteem by those who knew him It has been said that many went to see him as much for the boost in spirit as for the medical prescription (Alabama Reunion Edition of the Heritage of Blount County, 1989). He had a love and understanding of people which marked him as a psychologist as well as a physician. The following postcard send to his cousin, C. Claude Moore, in 1907 is a good example of his fun-loving personality for which he was known.

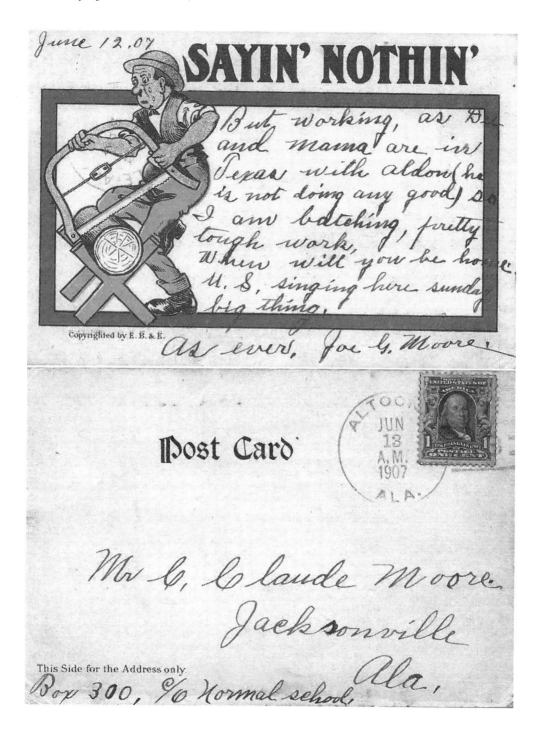

South Highlands Infirmary, shown above, was founded in 1910 by Dr. Edmond Mortimer Prince, Dr. David Sanders Moore, and Dr. Joseph Grover Moore (p. 65 Holley, Howard L. 1982.The History of Medicine in Alabama. University of Alabama, School of Medicine.) A history of Birmingham and Jefferson County published by the Jefferson County Historical Commission and the Public Library reported that this group headed by Dr. Prince raised 92,000 dollars locally and borrowed another 30,000 to establish the infirmary in 1910, The infirmary later became South Highlands Hospital. The hospital was acquired by HealthSouth and was HealthSouth Medical Center when UAB (University of Alabama in Birmingham) acquired the facility and renamed it to UAB Highlands as it is now in 2012.

A picture from the Fall, 2011 Alabama Heritage UAB shows Dr. Joseph G. Moore as being a member of the Birmingham Medical College, class of 1911 posing with the nurses from Hillman Hospital.

The Alabama Heritage presented an interesting story about the Birmingham Medical College (BMC). It was organized as a for-profit medical college in 1894. It was housed in a hotel by the name of Lunsford 209-211 21st street north, in Birmingham. In 1902, the college moved into a new building on Avenue F (later 6th avenue south) in the city's Southside between 19th and 20th streets.

In 1910, BMC was merged with Birmingham Dental College with a new name. The name was changed to Birmingham Medical, Dental, and Pharmaceutical College, and was still an independent for-profit school. However, sometime around 1912, the University of Alabama acquired the school and properties allowing all the enrolled students to complete their education (pp. 52-53 Alabama Heritage F 2011).

Joseph Grover Moore died July 20 1953 at the age of 65. His obituary reported that he died at home at his Green Springs Road residence. His death was due to complications from a circulatory condition that had caused him to experience ill health for several years prior to his death. He and his wife, Lucille Catherine Ford are buried in Elmwood Cemetery, Birmingham, Alabama. His wife, Lucille, who he had married on May 1941, was listed as his survivor along with nieces and nephews.

Dr. Joe G. Moore
Elmwood Cemetery, Birmingham

In ill health many years ---
Dr. Joseph G. Moore, 65, widely known doctor, dies
Headline from Birmingham News July 21, 1953. The
following is a partial excerpt from his obituary.
Dr. Moore was a member of the American Medical Assn., Southern Medical Assn, Alabama

State Medical Assn, Jeffers, Pemblon County Medical Society, Southside Baptist church, Birmingham Country Cub and held a life membership in the Birmingham Sportsmen's Hunting Club. ...In addition to his wife, he is survived by several nieces and nephews. Graveside services will be held at 4 p.m. tomorrow in Elmwood Cemetery, the Rev. John H. Buchanan, pastor of the Southside Baptist Church, officiating, and Johns-Ridout's directing. The family requests that no flowers be sent. Active pallbearers will be Walter R. Ford Jr., Edwin L. Moore, Ellis Dean, Gerry R. Terrill, Dan Moore, Howard Collins, Joe Vance, E, L. Greer and Stephen Dow. Members of the medical staff of South Highlands Infirmary and Birmingham Sportsmen's Hunting Club will serve as honorary pallbearers. Others serving will be Dr. James A Becton, the Rev. John Wiley H, Parker Osment, Ralph Dewberry, James R, Goetz, Major Wilson Ford, L Gordon Scaroro, B. L. Wilder, L. B. McWilliams, James W. Whatley, Walker Mattison, Milton Andrews, Edgar W, Stanford, John H. Walker, Frank Muse, W. Earle Hargrove, E. L. Camp, Robert A. Ashley Jr. White Gibson Sr., David B. Berry, L W. Gaines, Ivey Paris. E. L. McCain, Judge Clarence W. Allgood, Harry Pembleton and George Bramlett.

Home of Dr. Joseph G. Moore, Birmingham, Alabama

The other children of Dr. David Sanders Moore and Susan Moore were as follows beginning with their third child, Mary Pearl, who married Eugene Oliver Dean on January 3, 1901. Mary Pearl was born 12 September 1879 and died 16 January 1934. She and her husband Eugene Oliver Dean lived in Jefferson, Texas in 1910. In the 1920 census, they were recorded as living in Orange, Texas and by 1930, they were living back in Clarence, Alabama and Dr. David S. Sanders, Sr. was living with them. Mary Pearl gave birth to five children: Fannie Moore Dean, who married Meade Graves; Dr. John David Dean who never married and is buried at Oak Hill Cemetery in Birmingham; Lucille Dean, who married a lawyer, Mike Copass and lived in Seattle, Washington; Ellis Nunnalley Dean, who married Mildred Bradford, a first grade teacher at Susan Moore; and the youngest, Lillie May Dean, who married Sam Jones. Lillie May lived in Orange, Texas in the 1920s, but died in Reno, Kansas in 1985. Mary Pearl Moore Dean died in 1934 in Blount County, Alabama and is buried at Wynnville Cemetery.

MRS. E. O. DEAN DIES IN BIRMINGHAM

Mrs. Pearl Dean, wife of E. O. Dean, of Clarence, died in the South Highlands Infirmary, Tuesday night where she had been in ill health for some time but the direct cause of her death was a heart attack. Mrs. Dean was 53 years of age and was the only daughter of the late Dr. and Mrs. David S. Moore. She was a member of the Baptist church. The deceased is survived by her husband, two sons, Dr. J. D. Dean, of Birmingham, and Ellis Dean, of Route 2, Altoona; three daughters, Miss Lillie Mae Dean, a student at the University of Alabama; Mrs. Mead Graves, of Orange, Texas; and Mrs. Mike Copas, of Seattle, Wash; three brothers, Robert J. Moore, of McDade, Texas; Dr. D. S. Moore and Dr. Joe G. Moore both of Birmingham. The funeral services are to be held at Pleasant Hill church, (Wynnville) Thursday afternoon at one o'clock, with Wade in charge.

 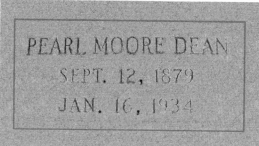

The fourth child of David S. and Susan Moore was Flavus M. Moore born 27 October 1881. He was 15 years old when he died on 14 January 1897. He is buried in Wynnville Cemetery.

The fifth child was Susan Florence Moore, born on 3 March 1883 and died when she was not quite a year of age on the 5 January 1884. She is buried in Wynnville Cemetery also.

Susan Florence Moore

The next two children were the medical doctors, Dr. Dee and Dr. Joe previously discussed. After those two sons, there were two more sons who died at young ages. The eighth child was Aldon O. Moore born on 18 March 1890 and died 24 September 1908 at the age of 18. The ninth child was a son Earl born on 19 of August, 1897. He died on 29 August 1899 just following his second birthday. He is buried in Wynnville Cemetery in the Moore family plot.

Susan Moore, the mother of nine children, survived only four of her children. It must have been a great heartache for her to have seen five of her children die before the end of her life. She died 1 Mar 1923. The following is her obituary that headlined her as a Blount County Pioneer:

> **Birmingham News, 1923**
> Mrs. Moore, for 50 years a citizen of Blount County died Thursday Morning at Clarence, Alabama following an illness of three years. Prior to her marriage 50 years ago, she was Miss Susan Nunnalley of Atlanta. Mrs. Moore is survived by her husband, Dr. David S. Moore; three sons, R. J. Moore of Austin Texas; Dr. David S. Moore, Jr. and Dr. Joe G. Moore of Birmingham; and one daughter, Mrs. E. O. Dean of Orange, Texas. She was also the mother of the late Prof. T. Clarence Moore of Birmingham. Funeral Services will be held at 11 o'clock Saturday morning from the residence. Burial will be in the family plot.

A death notice in memory of Susan Moore printed in The Southern Democrat and written by Georgia Hatley, her caretaker follows:

> **Mrs. Susan Moore**. On the morning of March 1st, 1923, the death angel visited the home of Dr. D. S. Moore, Clarence, and claimed the sweet spirit of his beloved wife. Mrs. Moore was an invalid for about three years-could not do anything and at times couldn't even feed herself the last month of her life. Mrs. Moore was a good Christian woman – loved by all who knew her. A good wife and mother. She never said anything about leaving this world except one time when Mrs. Moore and myself were talking about this life, and I said to her: "Mrs. Moore, I have had a hard time in this old world and I am trying to live a life so that when I leave this world, I will go to rest." And she began to cry and said, "Mrs. Hatley, I know you have had a hard time and so have I, so I am going to try to do as you said, I'm going to a better place than this." It is sad to think that Mrs. Moore is gone-never to see her again on this earth. I learned to love Mrs. Moore and I have sat and watched her day after day and didn't think she could live another day, but God knew best. She was really a mother to me. I loved her and I miss her so much. Her chair is vacant and no one can fill it. I can hear that call, "Come here, Mrs. Hatley, and help me up and would say, "I hate to be waited on". I told her that was all right, that I was ready any time I could help her.
>
> Poor old thing, we lifted her so much that her arms became tired. I didn't one time think that night when we put her to bed that she never would speak to me anymore. Oh, how I wish she could just talk to me one more time. Help me to live the life Mrs. Moore lived. I've been with her three years and I always found her to be a good Christian woman. She was so good and kind to those about her. Good mother and companion. Grieve not dear husband and children for Mrs. Moore is out of her suffering on this earth and is at rest. It is hard to part with loved ones, but I had to give up my dear mother, but I am going to see Mrs. Moore and mother again

someday; also all my dear loved ones. So children, let's all live so we will see your dear mother again. Dear children, this morning one month ago, at 2 o'clock in the morning the angels came and wafted the spirit of Mrs. Moore to a better place. Oh, how I miss her. It seems as if I never can get used to her being gone. It is so lonesome here. She sat at the window when able to be up and watched her chickens and tell me which ones she liked. Mrs. Moore is survived by her husband, Dr. David S. Moore, three sons and one daughter, and many relatives and friends. Written by one who loved her and cared for her so many days. Georgia Hatley.

Susan A. Moore, daughter of Jackson A. Nunnalley (25 Sep 1854 – 1 Mar 1923) Buried Wynnville Cemetery. (Copied from Death Notices from the Southern Democrat 1920 - 1927 p. 118)

Mrs. Susan Nunnalley Moore

Dr. David S. Moore

Susan's husband, Dr. David S. Moore lived almost 10 years after his wife's death. His obituary is excerpted here, as written in the Birmingham News in 1932.

SHORT ILLNESS IS FATAL TO DOCTOR
Moore Funeral Will Be Held At the Pleasant Hill Church Sunday
Funeral Services for Dr. David S. Moore, Sr. Route 2 Altoona, Alabama will be held at 11 a.m. Sunday at Pleasant Hill Church, Wynnville. Dr. Moore who was the father of Dr. David S. Moore, Jr. and Dr Joe G. Moore, part owners with E. M. Prince, of South Highland Infirmary, died Friday afternoon after an illness of several days at the infirmary.
Parents of Dr. Moore moved to Blount County from Georgia in 1863. Dr. Moore was graduated in medicine in Atlanta in 1879 and practiced in his native community for 50 years. He had retired from active practice four or five years ago. Dr. Moore is survived by one daughter, Mrs. E O. Dean, Altoona, Route 2; three sons, R. J. Moore, McDade, Texas; Dr. David S. Moore and Dr. Joe G. Moore, Birmingham; four brothers, Martin, Marion, John, and Dr. J. H. Moore, all of Altoona. Two grandsons, Dr. J. D. Dean, Birmingham; and Ellis Dean, Altoona, Route 2; and four granddaughters, Mrs. Meade Graves, Orange, Texas; Mrs. Mike Copass, Seattle, Washington; Mrs. Choice Smith, Austin, Texas; Miss Lillie Mae Dean, Altoona, Route 2. Relatives have requested that flowers be omitted.

Dr. David S. Moore and Susan A. Moore are buried at Wynnville Cemetery

Chapter 5

The Fifth Son of Robert M. Moore

Benjamin Martin Moore

Benjamin Martin Moore, (called Martin) who was born in 1854 and died in 1943. His wife was Havanna Frances Scruggs, called Fannie. Martin and Fannie were the parents of seven children. The Benjamin Martin Moore home was a charming structure with a story.

The Benjamin Martin home shown above, sat on Max Haynes Road at the location of the home where Ann Debtor Haynes Tidwell and her husband, Ronnie Tidwell now live. This Moore home was removed for the building of the current home by the J. A. Smallwood family, principal of Susan Moore High School 1942 -1965. The home of Benjamin Martin Moore has a unique history and was charming in architectural design. It was a large home due to its origin and original owner/builder. Dr. Joe Hendrix built an eleven-room house to be used as a hotel. A hotel in downtown Clarence, Alabama in 1889! Why would anyone build a hotel in this small community? It had been rumored that a railroad was to come near enough to Clarence that perhaps a train station would be here and the hopes were that there would then be a demand for a hotel. Disappointment came as the railroad was routed elsewhere. This was likely the Oneonta to Altoona to Gallant, Attalla and Gadsden route. When the railroad route was established in another location, Dr. Hendrix sold the house to Benjamin Martin Moore. It served him well. A few years after his father passed away, his mother, Nancy Jane Watson Moore moved in with him and his family.

The first child of this Moore family was *Oscar Jackson Moore* who died as an infant in the first year. Their second child was *James Robert Moore*, who was the owner and operator of Robert Moore's Store at Union Point.

J. Robert Moore's Store at Union Point after the business closed

J. Robert Moore was married to Annie Bentley. They had one child, a son, Edwin Leon "Red" Moore.

Red Moore on the porch at home in Oneonta 1940's or 1950's

Red Moore married Gussie Rasco. He eventually owned a large amount of the original Moore property in the Susan Moore area. His children are Betty Moore Ashley, Dan Moore, and Sallie Moore Pitts. Many of the burials for the members of this Moore family are located in Oak Hill Cemetery in Oneonta, Alabama.

Edwin Leon "Red" Moore acquired the Ford Dealership in Oneonta in 1934.

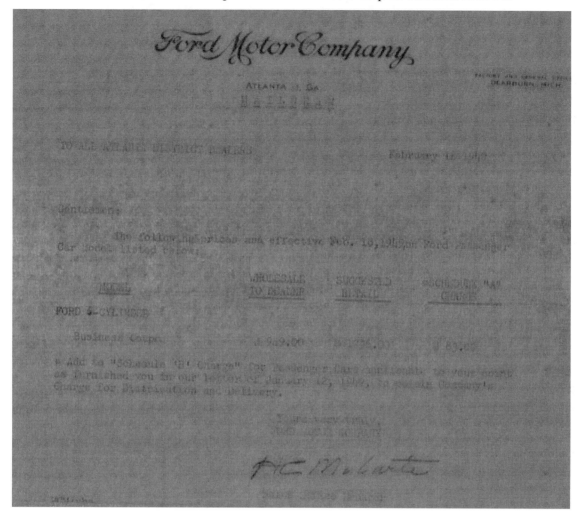

Red Moore receiving an award from Ford Motor Company

Edwin and Gussie's son, Dan, met his wife-to-be, Ann Hudson in Atlanta while playing football at Georgia Tech. Ann was living in Atlanta, modeling at the time. As a matter of fact, she was Miss Atlanta at the time. They began dating and married a few years later. In the first few years of their marriage they lived in North Carolina while Dan was serving in the Marine Corps. They moved back to Oneonta after Dan's time in the Marines and Dan joined Red in the Ford business at Moore Motor Co. in 1955. Ann and Dan had a daughter, Dana, in 1957, son Mike, in 1959 and son Matt, in 1962.

Dan Moore, playing football for Georgia Tech Dan is in the middle.

An ideal family - The writer of one of the several letters commending Oneonta Jaycees for nominating Dan Moore as their outstanding young man stated that Dan and his family could well represent Oneonta as Alabama's ideal family. They are pictured above: the older son Mike is with his father: Matt sits near their lovely mother, Ann. Standing is the boys' sister, Dana.

The Moore Family of Susan Moore, Alabama

In late 1964 General Motors approached Dan to buy the Chevrolet and Oldsmobile dealership in Oneonta which he did June 1, 1965.

Red and Dan Moore

Telephone 274-3741

208 Sixth Street, South

Oneonta, Alabama 35121
May 28, 1965

Dear Customer:

As you probably have heard or read, a big change is to take place at Moore Motor Company on June 1, 1965. The change can be very simply stated by saying that we will be known from that time on as Moore Chevrolet-Olds, Inc.

A move such as this is one that is not made in haste. We have proceeded only after a great deal of thought and consideration. General Motors is the world's largest manufacturer of automobiles and as their affiliate, we will be able to offer the people of Blount County and our customers everywhere, a greater variety of automobiles and trucks.

As our friends can attest, service has been our greatest concern for thirty-one years. We have endeavored to maintain a standard of excellence in our shops of which we could take pride. We will continue to carry Ford parts and service Ford products with special care.

We would not want to take the first step on June first if we had not expressed our gratitude to our very special customers for their patronage. Your friendship and business have meant much to us. We Moores hope to serve you for many years to come. In this respect, you know that we are sincere when we say that we do business to do business again.

If Moore Chevrolet-Olds, Inc. can be of help to you in any way, please do not hesitate to call on us.

Sincerely,

Dan R. Moore

In 1972 he was one of 18 dealers elected to the Board of Directors of the Alabama Automobile Dealers Association by the 387 franchised dealers. He was also voted by the 134 Chevrolet Dealers in the Birmingham Zone to represent them in dealer relations with the Chevrolet factory in Detroit. The Zone included Southern Tennessee, Alabama, and Northern Florida.

While Dan was busy managing the dealership Ann was busy raising 3 kids and doing her

Civic duty by serving on the Oneonta Parks and Recreation Board for several years and giving her time to and expertise in other areas such as arranging and providing flowers for Lester Memorial United Methodist Church and many, many wedding ceremonies.

Dan Moore's wife, Ann and their three children, Mike, Matt, and Dana

The whole family was very active in their church, singing in the choir and taking part on many leadership boards. Dana was active in music from an early age, joining the High School Band in Jr. High and becoming a Majorette in High School. Mike and Matt got involved in athletics in elementary school, taking part in whatever sport came next during the year. Both boys were named to the All-State football team their respective Senior Year. All three children attended and graduated from Auburn University. Dan sold Moore Chev/Olds in the early '80's when Mike and Matt chose to follow a different career path. In 1990, Dan died from an aortic aneurism. In 2003, Ann died in a house fire at her residence. They are both missed very, very much. Dana resides with her husband, Steve Langford, in Cape San Blas, Florida. They have two grown daughters, Mary Ann and Dagney. Mike resides in Vestavia, Alabama with his three children, son Gantt and daughters, Dailey and Charlie. Matt resides in North Shelby County, Alabama with wife Tammy Saunders Moore and daughters Elizabeth Ann and Amelia.

Dan and Ann Moore

Dan Moore and sons, Mike and Matt just before Dan died in 1990

Mike Moore recalled some memories of things his Pawpaw Red Moore told him. One was about his great grandfather, Robert Moore's store as he recalled the story was that due to fire or other reasons the store was located throughout the years on three of the four corners on that crossroads where it stood. Another story from his Pawpaw was that Red had bought dump trucks when he was only 14 or 15 years old and had law enforcement officers driving for him in their off time. Mike did add that he could not confirm that story! A third recollection was that Red had bought and operated a laundry/cleaners in 1928 when he was only 22 years old.

To conclude the story of the second child of Benjamin Martin Moore, J. Robert Moore and his descendants, what better way than to quote a son about his dad and Pawpaw. Mike Moore stated that Red Moore was the ultimate entrepreneur and Dan Moore was one of the most respected car dealers of his time.

The third child of Benjamin Martin Moore and Fannie Scruggs Moore was *Mary Ethel Moore* who married Jesse Burns. Ethel and Jesse had four children. Merle who married Walter Majors; Clara Burns, who married Joe B. Gunnels; Jerome J. Burns, who married Evelyn White; and Martha Francis Burns who died the year after she was born in 1919.

The fourth child of Martin and Fannie was *Ola Frances Moore*, wife of Eldridge Daily The children of Ola Frances and Eldridge Daily are Max Daily who married Jean Ingram; Dorothy Daily who married Charles Formby; Drexel Daily who married Doris Walls; and Verrell Daily who married Goober Maynor.

Beulah Ennis Moore was the fifth child of Benjamin Martin Moore and Frances Scruggs Moore. She was born on October 15, 1895 and married Jasper Asbury Bynum, son of Asberry Bynum on September 2, 1917. They were married in the home of her parents in Clarence.

They lived most of their lives in Oneonta, with the exception of sometime during the 1920s and 30s when they lived in Tarrant and Clarence. Clarence was the home of her parents who had plenty of room during the depression years to have others living with them. Beulah and Jasper had four children: Ralph Moore Bynum (July16, 1918) and Robert Paul Moore (June 13, 1921) were both born in Oneonta while the daughters, Rachel Constance (October 11, 1925) and Frances Nan were born in Tarrant. All of their children spent the majority of their growing up years in Oneonta and graduated from Oneonta High School. A story captured from The Heritage of Blount County, Alabama, Volume 5 and included here states that "during the depression years while living without electricity in Clarence with Beulah's father, Jasper would fill the trailer with kids, hitch it to the Model T and haul the lot to the river for swimming. At Clarence, too, one of the lasting family expressions was born. Jasper had seen houses blowing away during his childhood, and as an adult he always had a storm shelter, whether the family storm pit or simply a hole in the floor to the underspace. He "led" the family to the shelter during storms, and once, bodily carried Grandfather Moore (Benjamin Martin Moore) who all the while protested, "Silly, silly, silly"." (p. 139 of Blount Co. Heritage, Vol 5). Jasper was orphaned at the age of 9, and his and Beulah's family became a special joy in his life. Jasper and Beulah have been called" beloved parents". Their son, Ralph married Sibyl Cole in 1944; then Robert Paul "Bob" married Norma Brown in 1947 and second married Linda Romberg York in 1996; Rachel Constance married L. D. Bentley, Jr in 1947; and Frances Nan married John M. Davis, Jr. in 1953. These marriages added to their family and also brought the joy of grandchildren. Jasper died on March 26, 1961. Beulah died on December 8, 1968.

Bob Bynum, son of Beulah Moore and Jasper Bynum was born on June 12, 1921, graduated as Valedictorian in 1938 at Blount County High School, and served in World War II. He worked with the Social Security Administration until his retirement at which time he and his wife Norma relocated back to Oneonta. Norma died August 19, 1995. Bob remarried and now, in 2012, he and his second wife, Linda live on Shuff Mountain in Oneonta

Rachel Bynum, (first daughter of Beulah and Jasper) and L. D. Bentley, Jr., reared five children, Danny, Bob, Emily, Terri, and Debbi. This family was involved in Radio in Oneonta for a number of years. L. D. Bentley, Jr. owned WCRL/WKLD radio station which had a variety of programming through the years. Danny Bentley and his sister Terri Bentley Lowry are likely the ones most recently remembered for their early morning programs.

Frances Nan, the fourth child of Beulah and Jasper Bynum, was born January 4, 1930. She has memories to share about living with Grandfather Moore. She was called "Little Fannie" by her grandfather since her grandmother was also Frances and called Fannie. So, Frances became Fannie Nan and that name stayed with her for many years. She graduated from the University of Alabama and became an English teacher for a while before being involved in a variety of businesses with her husband. She married John Merrill Davis, Jr. on August 6, 1953 in Oneonta. Through the years, they lived and worked in Nashville, Memphis, Baltimore, and Richmond. John and Nan had two children, Janan Marie born December 21, 1956 and John Merrill Davis, III born on September 6, 1959. These children married and filled Nan and John's life with children and grandchildren. I recall shopping with my mother when I was a young girl for shoes and fabric for a new dress at the store in Oneonta that was run by Rachel Bentley.

I remember buying a pattern, fabric, and all the sewing notions for a dress that my mother made and I modeled in a fashion show sponsored by the store possibly around 1957. The fashion show was held at the auditorium of the old Oneonta elementary school.

Markers for Benjamin Martin and Fannie Scruggs Moore shown above are in Mt. Moriah Cemetery

These five markers are in a family plot in Oak Hill Cemetery at Oneonta, Alabama

Chapter 6

The Sixth Child of Robert M. Moore
John Morgan Moore

John Morgan Moore first married Frances E. Cox (Fannie) on 7 November 1878. G. F Ballew performed the wedding ceremony in Blount County. Fannie was the mother of John's children. He married a second time to Emma Entrekin and later to Millie Griffin. John was born in Walton County, GA in 1855 and lived to be 79 years old. He died in August of 1935. He is buried in Mt. Moriah Cemetery. John Morgan Moore was also a farmer as were many of the Moore brothers and their father. He was remembered by some as having a big grey mule! He owned a large amount of land that he entered and received in the Susan Moore area. He owned a portion of sections 10 and 11 of Range 2 East, Township 11. He and Fannie had two sons.

The eldest son was Joel William Moore who moved to McDade, Texas and first married Roxie Pate. Roxie died in Texas in 1904. They had one child, a daughter named Roxie who died in 1929 of tuberculosis. Joel married the second time to Clem Dungar and they had two children, Joel Howard Moore and John Lester Moore. Joel Howard was born and died in 1910 when only a few months old. The elder Joel's second wife, Clem died before 1930 leaving Joel, a widower with only their youngest son, John Lester Moore. Joel had two wives and three children to die before his own death. His death certificate in 1935 gave the cause of his death as nervous exhaustion. Joel had worked as a clerk in the post office in Bastrop, Texas and was the Postmaster in the years immediately preceding his death.

The second son of John M. Moore was Marion Moore (1882 – 1908). He married Nellie Phillips (1888 – 1970). Marion's children were Eleanor Frances Moore and Marion Verbon Moore.

Included here is a postcard of McDade, Texas railroad depot. This card was written by Joel Moore. You will notice that Joel wrote of Dr. Davy coming after Aldon. This was shortly before Aldon died in 1908.

H. & T. C. Depot. McDade. Texas.   Pub. by D. C. Atkinson

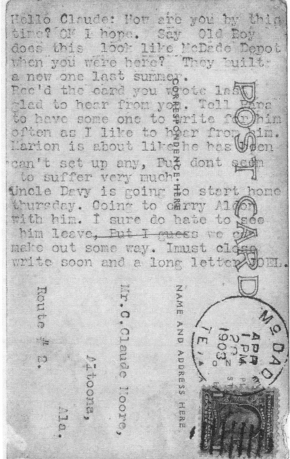

Hello Claude: How are you by this
time? OK I hope. Say Old Boy
does this look like McDade Depot
when you were here? They built
a new one last summer.
Rec'd the card you wrote last
glad to hear from you. Tell Pana
to have some one to write for him
often as I like to hear from him.
Marion is about like he has been
can't set up any, But dont seem
to suffer very much.
Uncle Davy is going to start home
thursday. Going to carry Alcon
with him. I sure do hate to see
him leave, But I guess we can
make out some way. I must close
write soon and a long letter DEL.

Route # 2.

Mr. C. Claude Moore,

Altoona,

Ala.

Chapter 7

The Seventh Son of Robert M. Moore

Dr. James Hamilton "Jimmy" Moore

The next child, the seventh son of Robert M. Moore and Nancy Jane Watson Moore was **James Hamilton Moore** (1858–1939). There is supposed to be something mystical about a seventh son; however, I think in order for that to be the case, the seventh son has to be the seventh son of a seventh son. With that being said, "tongue in cheek," we shall continue with the story. Jimmy, as he was called, was born in Walton County, Georgia, seventh son of a first son. As recorded in the 1860 census, Jimmy Moore was living with his parents and other siblings, (William T., Zachariah E., Robert B., David S., Benjamin M., John M., and Daniel M.) in Walton County. William T. died soon after the 1860 census. Jimmy was around eight to ten years of age when he and his siblings traveled with his parents in a covered wagon to Blount County. By 1870, Jimmy was about 12 years old and living with his parents in the Eastern half of Blount County. All children, with the exception of the eldest, William, were living with them in 1870. Two daughters had been born since the 1860 census, Nancy Elizabeth age 8; and Mary Emma, age 5. Jimmy grew up on a farm and followed the family tradition. His father, Robert M. Moore was always and only a farmer, both in Georgia and in Alabama. The domestic help N. A. Thompson, age 27 most likely came with the Robert M. Moore family from Georgia. She had been living with them at the time of the 1860 census in Georgia and was recorded with them in Alabama in the 1870 Federal census. She is not shown to be living with Nancy Jane in the 1880 census after Robert's death in 1877. His widow, Nancy Jane Watson Moore continued to live at the home place in Township 11, Range 2E in Blount County. The home later became the home of Dr. Jimmy and later on his son Carl lived there. The home was west of the school on what is now Susan Moore Road.

James Hamilton Moore and his 3rd wife, Savannah V. Bynum

The children living with Nancy Jane Moore, widow of Robert M. Moore in 1880 were James Hamilton "Jimmy" who was 21 and still single; Daniel Marion 20; Nancy Elizabeth, 18: and Mary Emma 11. The next year, on the 17th of February, 1881, James Hamilton Moore married Leila Isadore McDonald, the daughter of Thomas Kenzie McDonald and Louisa Jane Rainwater. The wedding ceremony was performed by G. F. Ballew, Minister of the Gospel in Blount County.

**Dr. James Hamilton Moore and wife, Leila Isadore McDonald Moore
and their 1st child, Charles Claude Moore**

Charles Claude Moore was the first child of Jimmy and Leila, born 15 January 1882. The second child was Alice M. Moore, born in 1884 and died in 1885. The third child, another girl was born in 1885 and died the day of birth. She is buried next to Alice in Mt. Moriah Cemetery. Her marker simply reads Infant 1884-1885. Leila Isadore died in 1886, the 18th of March. She is buried near the daughters at Mt. Moriah Cemetery. Her death left Dr. Jimmy with a four year old son to rear alone.

(Tin type from C. Claude Moore's collection)

**The picture above is James Hamilton, Leila Isadore and children,
Charles Claude and Alice Moore**

Alice was the first person to be buried in Mt. Moriah Cemetery

By 1888, Dr. Jimmy married for a second time to Eleanor Elizabeth Ray (1869 – 1890) daughter of Moses Ray and Elizabeth McDonald. Eleanor's mother, Elizabeth McDonald was a sister to Dr. Jimmy's first wife, Leila McDonald. Only one child was born to this marriage, Leila Ladora "Dora" Moore (14 May 1890). Eleanor died when the baby, Dora was 8 days old, 22 May 1890. Once again, Dr. Jimmy was left to rear young children alone, this time, a baby daughter, Dora and an eight year old son, Charles Claude. Jimmy married a third time to Savannah V. Bynum, daughter of Isaac Bynum and Mary Jane Reid Bynum. Savannah was born in Dec 1870 in Alabama and married Dr. Jimmy in 1891 at the age of 21. She was the widow of John Jordan, a saw miller, who had died in a sawmill accident in 1890. According to the census, she had given birth to six children by 1900 and only three of them had survived. She later gave birth to three other children.

The three surviving children of the first six born to James H. and Savannah V. Moore were Susan A. "Susie" Moore, born 1895; James Carl Moore, born 1897; and William Cleo Moore; born 1899. Living with the James Hamilton Moore family in 1900 was Mary J. Bynum, age 69, the mother of Savannah. She was the widow of Isaac Bynum. Children born to James H. and Savannah after the 1900 census were John David "J.D" Moore (1900–1971); Valula Pearl Moore (1903 – 1906); Robert Cayce Moore (1905 – 1984); and Coy O. Moore (1911 -1914).

C. Claude Moore, the first son of Jimmy and Leila was still living at home with his father and step-mother, Savannah in 1900 at the age of 18. Also, living with them was Dora, age 10, the daughter of Jimmy Moore and his second wife, Eleanor E. Ray. Claude like many of the other Moore men attended Blount College and also attended the State Normal School as it was known then at Jacksonville, Alabama. It is now Jacksonville State University.

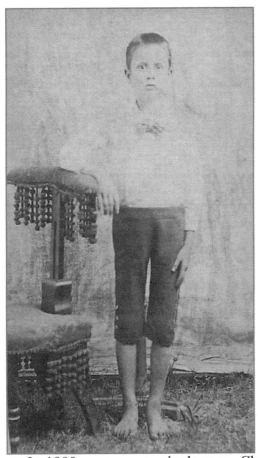

**C. Claude Moore - 4 Jul 1890
at Wynnville**

In 1900, as a young single man, Charles Claude Moore began teaching from school to school within the community. He taught for forty years, mostly in Blount County but a couple of the earlier years were in Georgia. He taught at Loganville, GA near Stone Mountain. Since Loganville is near the area where the residence of Robert M. Moore was located during his years in Georgia, it does make one wonder what the connection might have been that led my Grandfather Claude to that area. I never heard him speak about family located in that area at the time he was teaching there but that is likely to have been the case. Claude married in 1910 to Ada Ethel Lamb, daughter of James Sanford Lamb and Margaret Rebecca Scruggs Lamb. Claude and Ada lived at High Mound in their small rustic home until their new home in Susan Moore was completed.

Claude and Ada's new home was located on the east side of Highway 75 just north of the present location of the Susan Moore Town Hall. James Sanford Lamb (Ada's father) and his sons built Claude and Ada's new home.

Building C. Claude Moore's House. Claude is talking to his Father-in-law

Three daughters were born to them over the next ten years. Constance Ivaleen on 13 December, 1911; Leila Rebecca on 13 October, 1913, and Ada Ethel on 28 June, 1920.

Ada and Claude both taught school and the two older children were taken to school as very young children to sit at their mother's knee while she was teaching other children.

Claude taught many years in the Clarence School and then taught high school math at Susan Moore High School. He was often referred to as a "math wizard". He was among the first faculty of Susan Moore High School. All three of the daughters completed school at Susan Moore High School. Ivaleen, the first daughter of Claude and Ethel was among the members of the first class to graduate having completed all four years of their high school days after the school was named Susan Moore.

**Left to right back row: Rebecca Moore Miller, Ivaleen Moore Currey,
Ethel Moore Oden and Ada Ethel Lamb Moore
Front Row: L – R: Marie Currey and Janet Oden
Kneeling on the Left front: C. Claude Moore**

Ivaleen married Zolen Tracy "Rabbit" Currey in 1939. Rabbit coached and taught at Susan Moore High School in the 1950s. Ivaleen and Rabbit had two children, Ralph Tracy Currey and Marie Currey Jackson. Both were Susan Moore graduates and lived in the area most of their lives. Ralph was a medical lab technician, having worked for Dr. J. L. Wittmier, the Blount County hospitals, and for many years for Dr. Lennie Gibson at Snead. Marie was a teacher/counselor at Douglas High School in Marshall County, Alabama ending her career as a college professor at Jacksonville State University and The University of West Georgia.

The second child of Claude and Ada was Leila Rebecca, who married Connie Miller. Rebecca and Connie lived in the Miller settlement, north of Old Snead in Blount County all of their married lives. They had three children, Roy Wesley Miller, Glenn, and Elaine Miller Sisson. Roy became a lawyer, and both, Glenn and Elaine taught school until their retirements.

Ada Ethel Moore married Renfro Oden and they were the parents of Janet Oden Rodham and Charles Oden.

Ethel Moore Oden born 28 June 1920
Photo by Max Pate, 2012

Ethel graduated from Susan Moore High School in 1938, attended Snead State College and Jacksonville State Teacher's College. Ethel currently lives in Alabaster, Alabama with her daughter, Janet. She lived in Huffman, Alabama on Meadowbrook Drive for most of the time she was rearing her children and for many years afterwards. She and her husband, Renfro attended Huffman First Baptist Church where Renfro was a Deacon and Ethel was active in the church. Renfro worked for Chicago Bridge and Iron until his retirement. He was an avid hunter and grew beautiful dahlias for a hobby. Renfro is buried at Jefferson Memorial Cemetery in Trussville, Alabama.

Picture of Claude Moore with some of his Susan Moore Students

First Faculty of Susan Moore High School
Claude Moore, Jewel Stephens, Zula Eller, Daisey Reid, Virgie Wade
Back: W. A. "Gus" Moore, Principal

Professor C. Claude Moore pictured below

School Days
1944 - 45

He ended his teaching in 1947 at Susan Moore. Just to give a little insight to the number of small community schools in and surrounding the Susan Moore area from 1900 until Susan Moore began to grow into a more comprehensive school; the following list of the schools in which Professor C. Claude Moore taught over his lifetime is provided. From his own handwritten note, he taught at Mt. Hebron, Clarence, Concord, Harmony, Pine Grove, Altoona, Union Point, High Mound, Wynnville, Mt. View, Hendrix, and Susan Moore. Education has been a career field for many members of the Moore family. There are several living descendants of James Hamilton Moore who have taught school until retirement.

C. Claude Moore and family in front of their home

Daughters of Claude and Ada Moore: Ivaleen, Rebecca, and Ethel

Moores and Lambs at a funeral or family gathering

C. CLAUDE
JAN. 15, 1882
JULY 5, 1962

ADA ETHEL
OCT. 31, 1883
JULY 22, 1950

Dora, the only child of Jimmy and Eleanor Ray Moore married Warren Holland. For many years, this couple lived in the heart of Susan Moore on the road now known as Ridgeway Road. The Warren Holland home was a part of the Moore Farm and Warren worked on the farm and also ran a steam engine at the mill for one of the Moore's.

Mr. and Mrs. Warren D. Holland

The pictures above are children of Dora and Warren Holland and Claude and Ada Moore

J. B. Holland   Ray K. Holland

Grady Holland   L. S. Holland

Four Sons of Dora and Warren Holland served in four different branches of the military during World War II

Dora and Warren Holland reared a large family in their home along the road that led to the heart of Clarence or as some claim today it is the very heart of downtown Susan Moore. It is the home standing just beyond the curve of the road past the present home of Joey and Karen Bailey. The children of Dora and Warren were W. Grady Holland; Ray Kytle Holland, James B. Holland; L. Sanders Holland; Cleone Holland; Avonell, Everett "Pug" Holland; Mary Holland. Four of their sons were in various branches of the military during World War II. They were Grady, Ray Kytle, J. B., and Sanders. All were fortunate enough to return home safely. The Holland children grew up in Susan Moore, graduated from Susan Moore High School and being so close in age to other children in the community there were many good times.

J. Carl Moore, one of the sons of Dr. Jimmy and Savannah, with his wife, Pernia Light Moore lived at the home place of Dr. Jimmy Moore until Carl's death. Pernia remained at the home place as long as possible preceding her death. The original home was located west of the Susan Moore High School on Susan Moore Road, County Road 34.

Carl and Pernia were the parents of two sons, Talmadge and Jimmy Carl Moore, Jr. Talmadge married Carolyn Hullett and they had three children.

Talmadge and Carolyn are both deceased and buried at Mt. Moriah Cemetery. Jimmy Carl married Jane Brock, now deceased and they had one daughter, Teresa Moore Ashworth Lindsey who taught at Susan Moore until her retirement.

Robert Cayce Moore was one of the younger sons of Dr. Jimmy, who spent the majority of his years as a farmer, but also served in the military.

His wife, LeMerle Moore, is remembered by many as their Social Studies teacher. She taught many years at Susan Moore High School from 1925 until her retirement.

Robert and LeMerle had one son, Bob Moore. Bob is married to Betty Posey and they are the parents of sons, adding three more sons to the Moore family descendants!

This next section is about growing up in Susan Moore as a grandchild of Dr. James Hamilton "Jimmy" Moore.

LeMerle and Robert Moore   **Bob Moore**

Growing up in Susan Moore submitted by Bob Moore

My Dad, Robert C. Moore, was the youngest surviving child of Dr. James (Jimmy) & Savannah Bynum Moore. I was born after the death of both my Granddaddy and Grandmother – they died approximately a month apart. Dad related a lot of stories about them during my "growing up" years. In the last two to three years of high school, Dad and I mowed Mt. Moriah Cemetery, which is where my grandparents were buried. During that time, Dad would relate stories about them. One that I remember best is that my Granddad's second wife had died shortly after giving birth to the only child that they had together. The ironic thing about this is that my Grandmother's first husband had been killed at a sawmill the very same day that Granddaddy's second wife died. They are both buried at Mt. Moriah and the graves are relatively close to one another, probably because at that time, there were very few graves at Mt. Moriah.

Dad had dropped out of school before finishing because he was the last sibling still at home when Granddaddy had a stroke. He was forced to keep the farm up and help take care of Granddaddy and Grandmother.

Dr. Jimmy Moore, Robert C. Moore, and Savannah Bynum Moore

Granddaddy had been a traveling dentist. He received his dental degree from the Medical and Dental Departments University of Tennessee in Nashville, Tennessee. Dad said that he would travel around, by horse and buggy, and do whatever dental work a person would need to have done at the person's home. It was not unusual for him to pull all of a person's teeth one day, spend the night with them, and make them a new set of teeth the next day. I remember Dad telling me that as late as the mid 70's, there was a cousin of Dad's that was still wearing a set of teeth that Granddaddy had made. I still have a copy of one of Granddaddy's ledgers that he kept for payment records. There are several entries in the ledger that indicate that he either filled a tooth or pulled a tooth and the payment was two chickens or some vegetables or some other farm product. I am sure that the reason for this is that some of the people could not afford to pay money for their dental work, so they used farm products to barter with. Sometimes I think we may be better off today if we did the same thing. It may make us appreciate things more.

I have many more memories of growing up in Susan Moore. One of my favorite things to do was to ride my bicycle down to see Uncle Carl and Aunt Pernie Moore – they lived in the old home place where Dad and Uncle Carl grew up. It was always fun to get up in the attic of that old house and see what was up there. I remember that there was an old crank record player and only one record. I would play that one record over and over – it was "Turkey in the Straw".

Uncle Carl and Aunt Pernie's youngest son Talmadge had a train set that had been left there while he was in the service. Aunt Pernie would occasionally let me get it out and play with it – I remember it had a pill that you could put in the smokestack and smoke would come out of it. That always fascinated me – of course trains still fascinate me today, even to the point that I have gone out and purchased model trains to play with in my second childhood. Uncle Carl peddled eggs in Birmingham on Thursday (I believe that is correct) of each week. The early part of the week was spent in preparation of that Thursday trip to Birmingham and one day they spent "candling eggs" in a small building they called the Egg House. What that meant is that in a very dark room, they had a cardboard box that had a light in it (the only light in the room) and this box had a couple of small holes (about the diameter of the small side of an egg) in each side of it. Uncle Carl and Aunt Pernie would sit across from one another and put eggs in the holes and because the light would shine thru them, they could actually see into the egg and tell if it was either bad or if it had a chicken almost ready to hatch. This was the method they used to cull out eggs that was unsellable. I occasionally visited them on the day that they did the "candling" and they told the story about the day that I locked them in the Egg House and went home. They called for me to unlock it, but I had already left. Uncle Carl had to climb out of the window to unlock the door. I can't remember if I got in trouble about this episode.

Growing up directly across the road from the school provided other interesting things in my life. With Dad at home, because he farmed, and Mother at school, as a teacher, it was pretty difficult for me to skip school. Some of my closest friends escaped and did that, but I was always afraid that if tried it, I would get caught. The other difference from all my friends was the fact that I never rode a school bus to school and they couldn't believe how excited I would get about riding the bus when I would go home with them to spend the night.

I can remember as a little boy (probably 4 or 5 years old) that the Sloman family lived on the other side of the school and I liked to go and visit them. Their children were older than me – Duran was probably 10 years older and Annese was at least eight years older. I was scared to walk across the school ground alone, because I thought a bad "booger" lived in the boiler room of the school, because of all the strange sounds that came out of that boiler room. I can remember standing on the side closest to our house and hollering for Annese to come and get me. She would always come and when I was walking with her, I wasn't scared.

Dad was always a practical joker and I was sometimes a victim of his antics. I have heard many stories of how he would get my older cousins, Jimmy and Talmadge to fall for his practical jokes. I can remember one time that Dad had my friend Bill Hicks and me up at the barn and he had a new calf. He told us we needed to shake hands with that calves back leg. Bill wouldn't do it, but I wasn't going to let it scare me. Needless to say, that calf kicked me completely out of that stall and Dad had a good laugh at my expense. Growing up in Susan Moore will always be a wonderful memory for me.

University of Tennessee at Nashville, Medical and Dental Departments

James Hamilton Moore's graduation class from dental school is pictured above. The picture was contributed by Bob Moore. James Hamilton is almost in the middle of the picture on the second row from the bottom. He is the 14th person from the right of the picture directly by the side of the man looking to his left. Many stories have been told about how he loaded up his dental tools and traveled to where he was needed. His dental practice was similar to a "rolling store", only in his case; he was a rolling dentist, carrying with him whatever might be needed to do the dental work in the area. He did do some of his dental work at home, making dentures and even pulling teeth on the porch. The picture below is the back porch of his home.

The census records through the years listed him as an owner of his farm and in his earlier years his occupation was given as dentist; later years he was listed as a retired farmer. He died on March 27, 1939. The writer of his obituary stated he had been a fine dentist until a stroke some 16 years before his death. The stroke had hindered his dentistry work. His wife, Savannah, also died that same year only a few weeks after him, on April 16, 1939. They are buried at Mt Moriah Cemetery near Friday's Crossing, in Blount County.

Mt. Moriah Cemetery

Dr. James H. Moore and wife, Savannah

Obituary

PROMINENT CITIZEN DIES
From the Southern Democrat 1939

Dr. James Hamilton Moore died at his home on Route 2, Altoona, Monday, after several days illness with double pneumonia. At one time Dr. Moore was a very fine dentist, but about sixteen years ago he was stricken with paralysis and never completely recovered.

Dr. Moore is survived by his widow, Mrs. Savanna Moore, who is now very ill; five sons, C. C. Moore, Route 2, Altoona, J. C. Moore, Rte 3 Blountsville, W. C. Moore, Tarrant, J. D Moore, Birmingham, and R. C. Moore, of Route 3 Blountsville; two daughters, Mrs. W. D. Holland, of route 2 Altoona, and Mrs. E. L. Eller, of Atlanta, Ga; two brothers, B. M. Moore, of Rte 2 Altoona, and D. M. Moore, of Rte 3 Blountsville; eight grandsons, nine granddaughters and one great grandson. The deceased was eighty-one years of age and a member of Mt. Moriah Primitive Baptist Church at which place the funeral was conducted Tuesday by Revs. Ed Graves and J. L. Burke, with Robinette in charge.

Ada, Rebecca, Ivaleen, and Claude Moore.

Ivaleen Moore

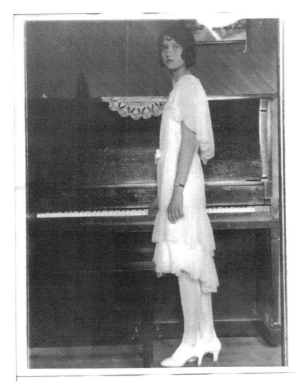

Rebecca Moore

Chapter 8

The Eighth Son of Robert M. Moore

Daniel Marion Moore

The next son, number eight was Daniel Marion Moore, called Marion. His wife was Marie Olga "Malzie" Green. He, too, like his father and brothers became a farmer and also did millwork. His children were Vester who married Samuel Alexander Murray; Oscar, who married Docie Blackwood; Bennett who married Cornelia Sloman; and Vernice C. who married Herbon White. These five children and their spouses added to the Moore family tree. Looking over the family tree, I certainly remember the house that Bennett Moore lived in on Susan Moore Road. Bennett was born Jan 18, 1904 and lived until November 7, 1957. His wife was commonly called Neil, short for the name Cornelia. Bennett and Neil had two children, a son, Arnell Moore and a daughter, Wondaline. Arnell married Mildred Niblett and added two daughters to their family, Nelia Sue and Betty Gale. Wondaline married Gerald Ridgeway. Gerald Ridgeway was a Boy Scout Leader and established a troop of boy scouts in the Susan Moore area during the mid-50s. Their son Larry Ridgeway married Margo Thomas.

Marion and wife, Malzie are buried at Mt. Moriah Cemetery

A day in the backwoods.

Chapter 9

The Ninth child and First Daughter of Robert M. Moore

Nancy A. E. Moore Adams

At long last, a girl was born. She was named Nancy Ann Elizabeth Moore, born August 13, 1861. She married John Quincy Adams. No, not the President John Quincy Adams; however, this couple had enough descendants to have had their own dynasty!

As an aside from the main story: you may recall that a domestic helper possibly traveled to Blount County with the Moore family, she was Nancy A. E. Thompson. Records show that the domestic helper was born in 1843 in Georgia. She remained with Robert M. Moore's wife until Robert died. The domestic helper, Nancy, later married and lived in Blount County until her death in 1915. It is possible that Robert and Nancy named their first daughter, Nancy Ann Elizabeth for this loyal domestic helper.

Nancy Ann Elizabeth Moore (19 Sep 1862 – 22 Jun 1891**)** died at the age of 29, a young mother of five children, Dona, Nancy Lee, Eugene, Labron, and Sallie.

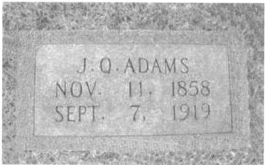

John Q. Adams

Her husband, John Q. Adams married the second time to Canzandy Smith in 1892 and she gave birth to more children who became a part of the Adams family. Of course, Canzandy helped to rear the older children of Nancy A. E. Moore.

The children of Nancy and John Adams were: *Dona Pearl Adams* (25 Jun 1882) who married Charles Hezekiah Harvey. This couple had five children, two died in 1919 as young children, ages 2, and 5. The eldest child of Dona and Charley was Attice Lola Harvey who married Mack Shelton. Harvey Lee Shelton, a son married Delores Pullen of Altoona, Alabama. Brady Cordell Harvey, the second child of Dona, a son born in 1911, lived to be 95 years old. He lived on Susan Moore road at the curve near the Park and was married to Bernice Waid, long time teacher and librarian at Susan Moore High School. Mrs. Bernice was remembered by many as a youth Sunday school teacher at Mt. Pleasant Baptist Church. They had one son, James Cordell Harvey who first married Shirley Southern. The third child of Dona was Wilburn Tressie Harvey who married Elizabeth Simmons.

The second child of Nancy Adams was *Nancy Lee Adams* bon Sept 7, 1883 and died on May 9, 1887, not quite four years old.

Eugene Adams, (1885 - 1975) the third child of Nancy Ann Elizabeth Adams married Lettie Belle Tidwell. Reid, Spud, Hubert, Lucy and Lydoth were the children born to this couple. An interesting aside to this story, from this author: I had heard of Reid Adams, a cousin of my grandfather, Claude Moore; but that is all I knew about him. So, one day a friend of mine who I had only known for a few years saw a copy of my family tree on my desk. She pointed out that Reid Adams was her step-grandfather for he had married Kate Lowery who was her grandmother. My friend, Sheilah Jordan told me that Reid Adams was the only grandfather she had ever known. She shared some funny stories with me. Sheilah told of her mother giving Reid a gift. He had moved to Texas and was raising long horned white cattle. Since Reid was a big talker and always had a story to tell possibly with embellishment, his step daughter, Dot bought a statue of a long horn white bull with a sign on it that said, "The Bull in this house goes on forever". Of course, he loved it! It suited his personality just fine! Sheilah and I are not related; but this just shows what a small world it is when it comes to genealogy. She could provide information about some of Reid's siblings that I did not know. For example: Lydoth Adams, who married Douglas Steffanauer and also lived in Texas was someone who was familiar to my friend. She knew her children: Douglass Steffanauer, Jr. who married Julie Cunningham; Danny Steffanauer, who married Judy Young and David Wayne who was nicknamed Butch. These are all descendants of the Moore family and were more familiar to my friend than to me.

Other children of Eugene Adams included Spud, Lucy, and Hubert. Spud married Maurine Talton. They had two children, Joan and James. Joan married L. D. Corbell. Three children, Craig Allen, Donna Joe, and Bryan were born to the Corbells. James Earl Adams had two daughters, Karen and Lois Adams. Eugene and Belle's daughter, Lucy married Claud Gibbons and they had no children. Their son, Hubert married Minnie Terry.

Laborn Adams was the fourth child of Nancy Elizabeth and John Q. Adams. Laborn was born 19 Jun 1887 and died 2 Jul 1960. He was married to Maggie Lewis and they were the parents of nine children. From this family, many notable individuals and recognizable names have descended.

The children are:

> Gussie Adams who married Annie R. Jones
>
> Aldie Adams married Ethel Hill
>
> Ellis Adams married Eunice Sloman
>
> Mack Adams married Ila Doyle
>
> Corrine Adams married (1) Verbon Fountain (2) Golden Dendy
>
> Lena Adams married Delbert Beshears
>
> Jo Adams married Henry Brown
>
> Rector Adams married Eva Martin
>
> Pearl Adams married Teague

Each of the above children of Labron Adams and Maggie Lewis added many descendants to the Moore Family Tree. Just to touch on a few family descendants, I will be selective in discussing this group. Laborn's first child was Gussie, who married Annie R. Jones This couple had two children, Donald, and Maxie Sue. Maxie Sue Adams married Jack L. Rigsby. The only daughter of this marriage was Brenda Rigsby who married Robert Sullivan.

Another child of Labron and Maggie Lewis Adams was Jo Adams who married Henry Brown. From that family unit came Nadine Brown, the wife of Bobby Lamb and mother of Susan and Tim Lamb. Susan Lamb married Rickey Adams.

In addition to the Adams descendants, other names found in this family are Rigsby, Sullivan, Thompson, Smith, Larue, Mason, Stevenson, Webb, Doyle, Osborn, Nix, Hamby, Yancy, Herring, Atchley, Warnick, Ward, Fountain, Dendy, Beshears, Snell, Stewart, Patterson, Dupree, Murphree, Lamb, Martin, Teague, Bullard and others in more recent generations. Now, does this sound like Blount County, Alabama?

The fifth child of Nancy Elizabeth Moore and John Q. Adams was *Sallie Adams* who married Steve Barnes. Intertwined in this Adams-Barnes family of seven offspring are such surnames as Beshears, Kirby, Crump, Simmons, Thompson, Whitehead, Tidwell, Mooty, and Buice among others found in the more recent generations.

Chapter 10

The Tenth Child of Robert M. Moore

Mary Emma Moore Ballard

The last child of Robert M. Moore was Mary Emma J. (6 Aug 1864-12 Nov 1912) who married A.N. Bud Ballard. Mary Emma and Bud Ballard gave birth to one son who died as a young boy of less than three years of age. He was born 27 Sept 1887 and died 11 Feb 1890. This child is buried in Ebenezer Cemetery in Blount County. His name is recorded as Ernest A. Ballard in local cemetery transcriptions. Vida Jones was an adopted child of this couple.

The Robert M. Moore family grew a large family tree! Once all the children and grandchildren were marrying and bearing more children, the family names of the community seemed to all be linked to this one family, directly or indirectly. That, of course, was not exactly the case, but even today when you view the community as a whole you still find many who are linked to the Moore family tree.

This Moore story would not be complete without including a section about life on the farm as the Moore Farm was a centerpiece of the community and important to many people throughout the area.

This dug well with its shelter served the family of Claude Moore in Clarence.

Chapter 11

The Moore Farm

This section contains valuable recollections regarding life on the Moore farm contributed by Robert D. Sloman, Robbie Bryan, Max Pate and others.

The Moore Farm spread over some six hundred acres more or less and in the early years of its existence was totally dependent on and maintained by man, mule, and plow.

Considering the size of the farm and the nature of the farming this was quite a task. The doctors, D. S., Jr. and Joe Moore surely had big plans for their farm to be self-sustaining. For several years, the farm indeed, was self-sustaining as Dr. Dee and Dr. Joe had dreamed it would be. However, the ending of the war, along with the advent of local mechanization rapidly emerging in Clarence, Alabama soon took its toll on mule farming for the Moore brothers.

George and Lavada Sloman and Robert Duran
George and Lavada were parents of Robert Duran and Annise Sloman

This family standing in front of their home is representative of the tenant families and homes on the Moore Farm.

During the hey-day of mule farming on the Moore farm, each tenant family (and there were twenty to thirty tenant homes on the farm) was allotted thirty acres to cultivate on a percentage basis. This percentage formula was three-fourths of the cost, profit or loss for the tenant and one-fourth cost, profit or loss for the farm. The seed and fertilizer was figured in a similar manner. Many other land owners in the area probably used a different formula. The Moore farm provided all the necessary equipment such as plows, wagons, gear, harness, and the feed for the mules.

During harvest time, and following the harvest, each family could choose to work at a nominal labor rate for the farm. Most chose to work on the farm, especially when the various fruits from the orchards were ready for picking. Some of the tenant families chose to work elsewhere.

The share crop tenants as they were called grew mostly cotton and corn. There were many other products grown on the farm. For example, apples, peaches, pears, melons, peas, potatoes, and several grains were among those found on the farm. Many of the fruits, melons, and vegetable produce were taken to the Birmingham fruit and vegetable market by Mr. Simmons, the farm manager, or his son Leland. On occasion one of the tenants had the honor to join him. The young boys of the family always got a trip to the city. This was an exciting time.

George Yancey was a tenant farmer on the Moore Farm and also worked at the Gin

Mrs. Thelma Yancey, wife of George was ill in the summer of 1945. She was carried to Dr. Brown's Clinic in Cleveland and treated there, but was not getting better. Dr. Joe Moore sent an ambulance for her to go to South Highlands Infirmary for him to treat her for malaria and complications from child birth. She stayed in the infirmary for six days.

The invoice below shows the bill for the hospital stay. Dr. Joe waived his fees of $50.00 because

Mrs. Yancey lived on the Moore farm.

SOUTH HIGHLANDS INFIRMARY
BIRMINGHAM, ALABAMA

№ 31989

DATE 8-13-45 19

RECEIPT

RECEIVED OF _____

$ _____

FOR: _____

$ _____

SOUTH HIGHLANDS INFIRMARY

BY _____

In addition, to the farm acreage, and tenant homes, the farm included a gin, the brick store or Masonic Lodge (as it was referred to by some), barns, outbuildings, and the Moore Mansion.

Brick Store and Masonic Lodge being built in 1926

According to Bryan and Jenkins, 2010, the tenant homes were rented by farm managers and laborers. Some say there were 20 homes and others mention up to 30 homes on the farm. Some of the families living and working on the Moore Farm during the forties and early fifties were Mr. Arthur Simmons and Mrs. Sally Simmons (Farm Managers), their son, Leland and his wife Bertha Simmons, the George Nibbletts, Mr. and Mrs. Hugh Cuzzort and their daughter Alma, Mr. and Mrs. Frank Wood; The George Yanceys; the George Lancasters, the Homer Hogeland family, the Aubin Hogeland family; Mr. and Mrs. Johnny Burnett, the Carl Elrod family, the Ted Elrod family, the Floy Elrod family, the Jess Foster family, Mr. and Mrs. Alex Stevenson; Mr. and Mrs. Bennett Moore, the Joe Lewis Family, the Noah Mulally family and the George Sloman Family. George Sloman was a brother–in-law to Jay Ben Dempsey. Both, George and Jay Ben were accomplished carpenters for their day and did much of the work on the construction of the Big House, the antebellum type home referred to by some as the Moore Mansion. George was also good at masonry and built all three chimneys in that home. That large antebellum mansion stood on a knoll where Dr. David S. Moore's home had originally stood. The planning of the construction of this new picturesque home required the removal of the old home. A three room section was moved several feet east and for the time of the construction of the new home, Ellis Dean and his wife Mildred lived there. Ellis was the nephew to the doctors; he was the son of Pearl Moore Dean. The mansion was a two - story style home where the doctors slept when they came for a week end. Ellis and Mildred occupied the majority of the ground level when it was finished. A small apartment type building was built to the rear of the "big house" for the Drs. Joe and D's chauffeur, Dude. I never knew his real name, but he was called Dude. He was a very nice person to all, and on occasion would eat a meal at one of the tenants' tables. Few of us youngsters had ever seen a black man before knowing Dude.

The Clarence Gin Company was considered to be a part of the Moore Farm. However, the gin was owned by Annie Pettus Moore, the wife of Dr. D. S. Moore, Jr. According to Bryan and Jenkins, (2009) in their book, entitled *Out the Road and Around the Corner*, Mrs. Annie may have been the owner for business purposes only; but indeed she did handle many of the tasks of running the gin. She came and checked on the gin in a chauffeur driven car, smoking her cigarettes in a long holder. That was certainly not a common site in our Susan Moore community. These "sights" are part of the special memories related to the history of this town that will long be remembered by those who lived here during those days. The sights such as the long line of wagons filled with hand picked cotton, and in later years trucks pulling trailers in that line as well will long be recalled.

Sometimes there were children riding on top of that cotton on the way to the gin laughing and enjoying the day even though they had worked in the cotton fields and picked that cotton also. Those were the days when schools were closed for a cotton picking vacation! Bryan and Jenkins referred to the sounds of the gin and not living too far away ourselves, many of us who lived in the area can recall that consistent humming sound and the fact that it was not considered a disturbing sound but just a mark of the completion of the day's work.

The bales of cotton were being prepared to be shipped to warehouses and later factories for the making of many products. One could observe the ginning process from the upstairs level and many watched as their own cotton was ginned and baled. People associated with the gin in various roles included, A. L. Elrod, Red Moore, Walter Belton, and O. G. Murphree as Cotton buyers; Bert Haynes and J. B. Haynes were watchmen; Joe Bryan was the ginner for many years; Aubrey Weems, Blant Freeman, Aubrey, Homer, and Cecil Haynes were all truck drivers. Some of the others mentioned by Robbie Bryan, J. P. Webb, Noel D. Hamby, Willie T. Hamby, Ted Elrod, Lee Anderton, Robert Sloman, Peggy Bryan Jenkins as bookkeeper, Early Snell, and Bill Norris.

Managers of the gin were Alex Stevenson, Oris Martin, A. L. Elrod, Ellis Dean, and Joe Lewis (Bryan and Jenkins, 2009). The gin was sold to Edwin L. "Red" Moore as was a large portion of the Moore farm. The end of an era one might say came when the tornado of 1957 destroyed the gin and many homes were damaged or destroyed throughout the community.

Following the tornado, Ross Debtor bought the gin property and installed a granary.

Robert Duran Sloman described the Clarence Gin as a five head cotton gin where all the cotton grown on the Moore farm was ginned. During the peak of harvest, wagons lined the roads into Clarence for a half mile in either direction. Most farmers, from the surrounding area brought their cotton here. A Mr. Joe Bryan was the ginner and always kept the ginning operation running in a smooth order. It took some thirty minutes to gin a bale of cotton. Most farmers liked for their cotton bale to weigh around five hundred pounds. In order to have five hundred pounds of cotton, one needed twelve hundred pounds of seed cotton. The cotton seed was usually traded for the ginning cost and the cotton hulls were loaded back on the farmer's wagon and returned back home to be used for cow feed. Dr. D. S. had the farm hands construct a two wire telephone line from Oneonta to the Big House and also to the gin. Now, we are talking "high tech"!

There were other gins in the area in the early days; one owned by Mr. Blanton Freeman. His gin was a much smaller operation. The Moore Gin was destroyed by a tornado in 1957 and never replaced. After the farm was sold, Mr. Columbus Hood, or Red Moore bought the site. Later, Ross Debter built a granary, or feed mill there. If you look closely at the Feed Mill picture, you will recognize the white structure in front of the other buildings. It was the home of the first town hall of Susan Moore after the granary was no longer in business. The building has been used for a variety of purposes and is still standing today.

A saw mill was also a part of the farm and was used exclusively to saw lumber for tenant and farm use. The tenant houses were all old and required constant attention. Therefore, lots of the lumber was necessary for tenant and farm use.

In the beginning, we mentioned that mechanization added to the demise of the farming being done exclusively by man, mules, and plows. The mechanization on the Moore farm included a steel wheel model-H, international tractor that was used primarily to power the saw mill and pull a small combine. The combine was somewhat primitive as far as machines of today; the grain harvested was threshed and caught in cloth sacks, tied, and dropped to the ground, so as to be retrieved by hand, then loaded on wagons and carried to the grain barn. Two very large mules were used to pull the Dray wagon load of grain.

Dray Wagon

The purchase of a Model M-International tractor was to be for the sole purpose of pulling a thirty inch double disc turning plow.

Later a Model LA – John Deere Tractor was purchased for the purpose of pulling the spray wagons that were used in the orchards.

It was eventually outfitted with a five foot cutter bar mower that was to be used to mow the wheat, hay and etc. This little tractor replaced a couple of mule drawn mowers. This tractor was a very welcome addition as most of us youngsters were allowed to learn the skills necessary to pass a driving test.

The new mown hay was shocked or stacked around poles to cure in the sun. When it "cured out", it was loaded by pitch fork onto wagons built for hauling hay to the hay bailer. The hay was then fed by pitch fork into the bailer that was powered by mules. The bailer pressed the hay into some sixteen by sixty inch bales, about five feet long and weighing about eighty pounds. They were tied with wire and then stored in the hay barn ready for the livestock. The best hay was kept in a separate place to be used to feed the doctors' horses.

Around the end of WW II, Mr. Simmons encouraged the doctors to purchase a surplus military Jeep. This little jeep came with some type of new fandangle hitch that was designed to pull a flat bottomed turning plow. Mr. Simmons thought that since it was a four wheel drive, it was supposed to pull the plow. His idea did not work out and the jeep was assigned other duties. It was often used by the high school.

The Barns and Outbuildings on the Moore Farm

There were two large barns on the farm, a smaller horse shed, a large Corn crib and the cow barns at each tenants place. The mule barn, as we knew it, was a very large and tall Gambrel roof structure with metal roof and ship lap white painted wood sides. This barn was probably some one hundred forty feet long, one hundred feet wide and forty feet tall. The loft area was the size of the lower area. This particular barn was adorned with a metal track above the loft attached to the rafters, just under the roof. A traveling hay spear moved along that track from the rear to the front of the loft and dropped to the wagon on the ground to unload the load of loose hay. A mule was hitched to a rope that connected to the traveling spear by the arrangement of a series of pulleys and viola, the hay was soon in the barn. The wagon load could be unloaded in one lift.

There was a very wide hall in the center of the barn with mule stalls to the left. There was also a hall or entry way left of the stalls where the cattle were fed before the cow barn was built. The mule stalls were about fourteen feet wide and numbering probably twenty hay drops were so arranged as to allow for two stalls to be fed through the same – hay drop openings. Outside the stalls in the hall, hooks were attached and arranged on the wall so as to allow for the storage of the harness for that particular mule as everyone was different in stature. On the opposing side of the hallway were large rooms about half the length of the barn used for different purposes. The fertilizer, seed for planting, cotton seed meal and many other things wren kept there under lock and key. The equipment was kept in the remainder of this side of the barn. Near to this barn was a large crib. This building was floored and partitioned for the storage of grain, particularly wheat, oats, and corn. Immediately behind this building stood the small horse barn, used exclusively for the doctors' horses. Doctor D. had a special passion for the sport of fox hunting on horseback. Many Saturday mornings, he and Dude, his chauffer would arrive in Clarence to indulge in his sport.

Today, the farm is no longer in operation as it was in those early days. Various people now own the land. Some are growing timber, some have cattle on their portion, and some appear to be waiting for a golden opportunity in the future. All the original barns are gone; but, the last barn built to serve the farm is pictured here. This barn is still standing as you see it here in 2012.

An old barn on the Moore farm
Photo by Max Pate, 2012

More Memories of the Moore Farm and Growing up in Susan Moore

Max Pate

Max and Conrad Pate on their mule

In 1946, we moved to the Holland farm that previously was a part of the Moore family farm. I was six years old and starting to school at Susan Moore. This was the first house for us to live in that had electricity and it was originally the Warren and Dora Moore Holland Home.

A birthday party for children growing up in Susan Moore.
L to R – Bob Moore, Bill Hicks, Annese Sloman, (name unknown), Jerry Cardwell, Duran Sloman, Kermit Cardwell, Max Pate, Albert Lee Campbell, Fairy McElvany in back.

My father was a carpenter and worked on the Moore mansion when he was not farming. We had a large cotton and corn farm that we worked with a pair of mules. I remember going to the Moore gin with Daddy (Rex Pate) and it would take several hours for us to get our cotton ginned. The gin was a fascinating place for us to tour. Sometimes they would have a fire in the gin heads and have to stop the gin until they could put the fire out.

One afternoon after school, Mrs. Mildred Dean invited Joan Elrod, Elaine Morris and me to tour the Moore mansion. The house was built like the Mount Vernon style. It was the largest and most beautiful house we had ever seen. It had long windows in the living room and beautiful drapes that went to the floor. The couches were covered with the same material as the drapes. The long stair case had a landing halfway up and a large chandelier hanging from the ceiling from the upper level.

One of the things that impressed me was in the laundry room was an ironing board built into the wall that would fold up and had doors to conceal it. This was certainly not common in our locale at this time in history,

The Moore family was a great asset to northeast Blount County with their work as doctors, dentists, educators, merchants, millers, and farmers. They employed several people at the farm and gin during hard times throughout the depression era. It would be great if we could have preserved all the beautiful houses I grew up with in the 1940s and 1950s. Many of the homes were destroyed for progress and some accidentally burned. The Moore Mansion burned in the mid 1950s. Others deteriorated over time and were beyond repair.

Below are some pictures made on the Moore Farm near tenant's homes.

Robert Duran Sloman   **Annese Sloman**

**Back Row:
Huey Dean Dempsey and Carolyn Dempsey**

**Front:
Robert Duran Sloman, and Annese Sloman**

Reliving old Memories
L to R - Robbie Bryan, Kermit Cardwell, Jerry Cardwell,
Robert Duran Sloman and Max Pate (Photo made in 2010)

When these men were young boys they played in the woods behind where they are standing. All of them grew up in the Clarence/Susan Moore area. Kermit and Jerry lived just down the hill and over the creek from where my brother Ralph and I grew up. We had bicycle trails, go cart tracks, a tree house, and even homemade canoes to float in the creek. Down at the foot of the hill was a big flat area that we called down in the bottoms. Grandfather Claude Moore used to tell that it must have been an Indian Camp. I remember Ralph, Kermit, and Hollywood Goble (another lifelong Susan Moore friend now deceased) would camp out and dress up like Indians and look for arrow heads. Of course, I was little tagalong sister and I did not always get to be involved in all the fun and games. I remember that they sent me to the house to find out the time and it took me a while to figure out they were just getting rid of me! We did not have telephones until some of these guys had graduated from high school and moved on with their lives; so those of us who lived on the edge of the woods had our own code for contacting one another. We used to call it "blowing our fist". We could vary the sound with long and short whistles in a code that meant come over here or I am coming over there. We knew the other party had heard us when he or she responded. Those were the days!

Chapter 12

The Social Scene in Susan Moore

Social life during the 40's and 50's in Susan Moore for the men consisted of sitting around in a local store, perhaps on empty nail kegs, or straight-backed chairs with woven straw or rope seats. Sometimes the winter scene may have included a pot-bellied stove with people standing around talking while "wetting their whistle" by drinking a cola (one of those small 6 cent bottles). Of course, there was Church on Sundays for the whole family and special weekly meetings for various groups. The schools provided many activities for the whole family...plays, carnivals, talent shows, donkey basketball games, invited groups like the Harlem Globetrotters, and of course, the basketball and football games with standing room only. Susan Moore must have always had great enthusiasm for their Bulldogs; the team mascot for that enthusiasm remains today. Home Demonstration Club meetings were popular for women during the forties and fifties and into the early sixties at least. The young people were mostly dependent upon the Church youth groups to provide activities, such as picnics, swimming at a lake, skating events or other group trips to camps in the summer. The neighborhood young people were more likely to know and accept one another as all a part of the "group" than it seems in today's world when through transportation, communication, and the world of technology, teens reach out farther for their friends, and have access to so much more entertainment than was ever imagined by young people from the 1900s through the 1950s. Yet, now in this supposedly more advanced age, there are no movie theaters in our nearby local towns, no drive-in theater nearby as there was in the fifties, no cruising around the "Clock"! Of course, cruising around the clock was the common vernacular for riding again and again around the popular restaurant in Oneonta named for the popular song of the fifties, "Rock around the Clock". Today, instead of it being a fun thing to do and a way to meet friends, and sit in a safe area to visit with one another, teens might be ticketed for cruising or told to move elsewhere. Those were the "days" of fewer harmful elements in our society for young people to have to learn how to appropriately handle. Teens did congregate after school at some of the local stores at least to get a cold drink, chips, or a candy bar. Most either were walking or waiting on someone to come to get them following an after school-hours event.

Cars were not driven to school by very many until the sixties and even then that was rather limited. Girls rarely had their own cars! Oh, the signs of the times! Today, a girl in a family would be very upset if her brother was given a car when he turned sixteen; however, when she turned sixteen it was never even considered as a possible choice to buy her a car. Of course, there were a few exceptions that can be recalled of girls with cars cruising the roads on the weekends. Usually the cars were merely on loan from a brother, uncle, or dad; but I do recall one or two who had their own car! Wow!

With these thoughts in mind: businesses in the neighborhood provided much of the social opportunities as people went about their daily obligations; stores and the various churches met more than the supplying of groceries, farm supplies, and spiritual needs, and the various men's organizations, and ladies groups other than fulfilling their stated purposes were also social organizations, it is interesting to note that a lot of those elements have faded and for many, today's social mediums, such as Facebook, Twitter, texting, and emails are taking the place of local hometown "congregation". The Internet continues to grow and change the landscape of small town America. Even yard sales are beginning to be handled as online lists, auction sites, and recycled goods sites, sometimes even free items are listed.

Susan Moore, over the last fifty to sixty years, has had numerous stores and businesses, all of which added much to the community. Today for the most part those are no longer close at hand. Most people have to travel farther than they once did to meet their daily needs. However, is it possible that the nearest superstore or malls of the world have become the social arenas for many? Maybe so. But the old stores and the friendly familiar faces are hard to replace.

Chapter 13

The Store Fronts of Clarence

One of the earliest recalled stores in Clarence was that of J. Pete Phillips. Pete Phillips bought his store from Dave Hood (Susan Moore Reunion Book, 1989). Pete had moved to Clarence around 1908 and ran a store at the crossroads of Clarence. That crossroads is today's intersection of Susan Moore Road, Gilliland Road, and Max Haynes Road. Pete Phillips sold this property to O. C. Weaver around 1938 when his health began to fail.

O. C. Weaver's General Store

Oza Clifton Weaver and wife, Catherine Elizabeth Warren Weaver purchased a general store in Susan Moore in 1932 in front of and across the road from the Moore Mansion. This store was operated as O. C. Weaver General Merchandise from 1932 - 1948. The merchandise included a little of everything, such as groceries, shoes, overalls, fertilizer, coal, horse saddles, hardware, and roofing. Of course, there was candy and ice cream! Those were the "days" for candy bars and colas were only a nickel. The store was also a place of amusement as it contained a "Rock Ola juke box" in the store for music and a pin ball machine. What great fun for the after school crowd and how difficult it must have been to keep the students from sneaking over to the store during school hours. There was a one year period of time when it was leased to a Mr. Jenkins or Jennings. Mr. Weaver became ill while in service and was diagnosed with leukemia. After his military discharge the family returned to the store in 1944 and operated it until selling it to Wilburn Adams in early 1948. According to information furnished by the son of Mr. O. C. Weaver, Warren Weaver, O. C. had built several rooms onto the back of the store where the family lived while operating the store. O. C. and Catherine had three children, Margaret Ann, Doris Jean and Clifton Warren (better known as Buddy). The family sold the store and moved to Albertville and Mr. O. C. Weaver died from his illness in January, 1949. He is buried at Liberty in the Antioch Cemetery near where he grew up. O. C. was a Mason and a Shriner. His business was at the main cross roads of Clarence directly across the road (now, Max Haynes Road) from the Masonic Hall.

Memories of Wilburn Adams Store

Contributed by
Johnny Adams and Kay Adams Smallwood

We (Son and daughter of Wilburn Adams) think the store was purchased in 1948 and Kay was born in 1949. The early years were apparently very busy and Mother and Dad worked all hours. When people knew you lived in the back, they would just knock on the door and asks you to open up. Mother told many times that one Sunday morning someone got them to open and they were so busy they could not close. They were able to get everyone out by 10:30 and left for the hospital in West End and I, (Johnny) was born two hours after they got to the hospital.

Wilburn Adams store with Johnny Adams on the tractor

The property where the house is located, across the road from the store was purchased in 1956 and we moved into the house in 1957. For years, while we lived in the new house, people would still come to the house and ask us to open. Kay and I would take turns going to the store to open up for those customers.

Wilburn Adams, taken in 1938 before he owned the store in the background.

In the fifties and early sixties, we were busy with all types of customers. We had numerous small farmers who bought fertilizer, feed and seed. Many times we would get up early to load small truck loads of fertilizer. Ricky and I were used, when we delivered large loads of fertilizer, to keep the bags pulled to the back of the truck so the men could unload. We delivered fertilizer to most of the farms in area and a number of the people wanted it stacked in the barn loft.

In the summer, some of the farmers would go to Birmingham and get a truck load of young Black men and women to chop cotton. Several of those would come to the store at lunch and get small orders for lunch. We had stick bologna and hoop cheese, which we would cut to size. We would put the individual lunches into small (size 1 or ½) bags with a canned drink and dime pack of saltines. Some would order pork and beans or other small cans of lunch meat we kept in individual sizes.

Elbert Adams and grandson, Johnny Adams

During the short twenty years we operated the store, the changes are a snapshot of the way life changed in those twenty years. Business was extremely good in the 50s and early 60s, but began to trend downward rapidly in the late sixties. This was the change from the day when everyone had a small farm to everyone working in Birmingham, Gadsden or Huntsville and one or two large farmers renting most of the farms or buying out the farm altogether. We sold groceries to the majority of the people in the area until the mid 60s. Somewhere in the mid 60s, attitudes changed about many things. They were driving longer distances to work, so we became more mobile. People in the Susan Moore area would not think of driving the 10 miles to Oneonta during the week to buy groceries, or to go to the bank during the week. That was a Saturday event. We somehow grew to going to Oneonta or Albertville and did not think about it. By the time, we got to the 70s; it was not unusual to go to town three times a day.

I have always felt there was more of a change from the early part of the 60s to the latter part. They seem to be more than 10 years apart. An excellent example is the number of school kids who would come to the store after football or basketball practice to catch a ride home. In the early days, we had a large group who would be looking for a ride. Before a Friday night football game, Mother would make sandwiches for several players who had no way back to the school for the evening game, if they usually went home on the school bus. They would come to the store to "kill time" and then I think they caught on to the fact Mother would feed them.

The last two players, who did not have a car and needed a ride home, were in Kay's class. Two years later, when I was a senior, I cannot remember anyone who did not have his own car.

Wilburn Adams Store
Picture was contributed by Johnny Adams and Kay Adams Smallwood

Wilburn Adams Store stands out in this writer's memory for it was there that I went with my Dad, Rabbit Currey to purchase mother's grocery list. Dad always added a big chuck of cheese cut from the round cheese in the refrigerated glass fronted case. That is where the meats were kept as well. I remember that around Christmas time, Wilburn or perhaps it was JoRee who would add items that would appeal to the children. One Christmas, Dad bought this beautiful doll that stood three feet tall to give to mother. Well, she kept that doll in its box for the rest of her life as she did many other things! Of course, I wanted to play with her but "she was Mother's doll". So, I never did; but, I could look at her through the cellophane paper front on the display box. As was stated by Johnny and Kay, the Wilburn Adams family lived in the rear of the store for a few years and when the children were young, sometimes you could hear the children playing. Wilburn's store was across the street, (now Max Haynes Road) from what we have referred to in this book as the Brick store or Masonic Hall. In the fifties that building was used as Wilburn's feed and fertilizer store as was mentioned by Johnny. I (Marie) would go with my Dad to purchase chicken feed in order to pick out matching sacks to the ones we previously had purchased so Mother would have enough material to make me a new dress. Of course, Wilburn was not the first person to run a store at that location on the busy corner of Susan Moore Road and Max Haynes Road. He did not own the Brick Store at first but added it later. This building, the brick store as we know it, was originally built as a doctor's office, drug store, and the only post office ever located at Clarence. Wilburn later built a service station and dairy bar on State Highway 75 at Susan Moore Road. Later, Bruce McCray operated this store as a grocery and service station until 2011.

Wilburn Adams was a descendant of John Quincy Adams and his second wife, Canzandy Smith. Wilburn was born in 1916 and served in World War II. He married Frances Josephine Marie Scruggs in 1944. She was the daughter of William David Scruggs (1879-1949) and Arrie Eller (1880-1964) Wilburn and Joree as she was known by most everyone had three children, Kay, Johnny, and Rickey. Wilburn died in 1969 and JoRee lived until 2002. They are buried in Bethel Cemetery.

Other stores in the Clarence/Susan Moore area included the Riley Bryan store across the road from the gin/granary property. Riley Bryan and Oma Scruggs Bryan were the owner/operators of their family business, a grocery store "filling station". Riley surely planned it to be in a convenient location, near the gin and half way between the school and what is now known as State Road 75. It was a busy place during the ginning season. Riley worked on the Moore farm and later at TCI (Tennessee Coal, and Iron) in Ensley. Riley and Oma had two children, Peggy and Robbie. Mrs. Oma, Peggy and Robbie ran the store while Riley worked away from home.

Riley Bryan's Store with Oma and Robbie pictured above

Robbie had a little yellow jeep, "Nelliebell" that carried all of us boys for a ride on the back roads of Clarence. The Riley Bryan store was destroyed by the 1957 tornado, the same one that destroyed the gin and other homes in the area. Peggy Jenkins and Robbie Bryan still make Blount County their home and have written a book that has been cited in this writing to which you may wish to refer for more information about growing up in Susan Moore.

Moving a little farther to the east of the school, along Susan Moore Road, past the curve, and going on past the ball fields and park to the crossroads at Highway 75, Max and I can recall a number of stores and various owner/operators of those stores. This crossroads, it seems to me should be called The Five Points of Susan Moore since there are five directions of traffic coming together here – Wynnville Road (County 34), Bulldog Road, Susan Moore Road (Co. 34) and of course, the northern and southern directions of State Highway 75. Near the creek, Uncle Jim Lamb (as he has been referred to previously) built a store in 1929. He was Uncle Jim Lamb to the authors as well. He was a brother to Marie's Grandmother Moore (Ada Ethel Lamb) and a brother to Max Pate's Grandfather Gordon Lamb. Jim Lamb also owned a grist mill and a blacksmith shop at the end of Wynnville Road. After his death in 1934, Radford Ray and others owned and/or operated that same store. Beginning around the 1940s, the owner/operators were a Jim Barnes, Marie's father, Zolen T. Rabbit Currey, Lonnie Johnston, J. A. Smallwood, and J. B. Haynes. Marie's mother and dad ran the store there in 1939 after they married. They lived in rooms in the back of the store as seemed common in small rural general stores. Rabbit always told stories about owning a pig that would drink colas and people would come into the store to buy one just to have his pig drink it. Rabbit was an experienced store operator as he had relocated here from Albertville when he and Ivaleen married. He ran a store for several years on old highway 205 between Albertville and Guntersville. The location in Marshall County was named Rabbit Town after Rabbit. It is still known by that name today. However, after Ralph was born, the family moved to Birmingham where Rabbit worked at Tennessee Coal and Iron (TCI) during the war years until he began his career in teaching and coaching. Radford Ray, most likely was the next person to run that store. In the early 1950s, Mr. J. A. Smallood bought the store and named it the Bill Bob store for their twin sons. Their motto was "Bob Your Bill At The BillBob". Bill Smallwood still has a pencil with that motto on it that was used for advertisement.

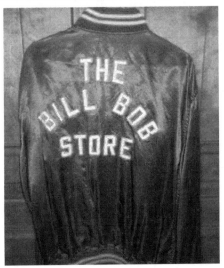

About 1958, Bill Haynes and his father, J. B Haynes bought the store and house from the Smallwood family. They removed the grist mill and built an automobile shop. The store and house was torn down in 1980 and a new house built on the property. Bill Haynes shared with Max that he saved the large plate glass windows from the store.

About two miles north of Susan Moore town hall on Highway 75, just passed Mt. Zion Church of God, Gordon and Willie Crump Lamb operated a general store and a grist mill. Gordon and Willie were my grandparents (Max Pate) and the great Aunt and Uncle of Marie Jackson.

Willie and Gordon Lamb's Store
Willie Crump Lamb on the left and Gordon Lamb on the right.

Front to Rear. Opal is holding her granddaughter, Martha Lou, Gordon Lamb and Willie Crump Lamb.

My brother, Conrad and I (Max) worked at Granddaddy's grist mill on weekends. We drove the truck to the Gadsden Curb Market on Saturdays to sell produce for our Grandmother, Willie Lamb.

Just next to the Claude Moore property, east on Wynnville Road was the James Sanford Lamb Home and acreage. He was the father of Gordon Lamb and thereby Max Pate's great grandfather.

James Sanford Lamb Family
Back: L-R, Will, Charles, Gordon, Ada, Golden
Front: James Sanford, Jewel, Margaret Rebecca, and Jim

He was also my great grandfather as my Grandmother Moore was Gordon Lamb's sister, Ada Ethel Lamb Moore. She was the eldest child in the family. An early gin and saw mill were a part of this farm. James Sanford Lamb's family was very industrious and one might say gifted carpenters

James Sanford Lamb, far right with four sons, Will, Jim, Gordon, Charles and two children

James Sanford Lamb's farm joined the Moore farm on the west side. He built a two-head gin and operated it for several years before the Moore gin was built. This was before electricity was available in Blount County. It was powered by a large steam engine. Ronald Kent told me (Max) that great grandfather Lamb bought a steam engine and had it shipped by train to Altoona. He had to build an extra large wagon to haul it to Clarence. The concrete pad is still there on Wynnville Road where the engine was mounted. It also powered a saw mill that was used to saw and mill the wood for the houses he built for all his children when they married.

Chapter 14

Early Churches and Cemeteries in the Susan Moore Locale

Mt. Moriah Primitive Baptist Church

Mt Moriah Cemetery is located near Friday's Crossing within the area of the current town of Susan Moore. The Mt. Moriah Church was believed to be the oldest Primitive Baptist Church in Blount County. It was constituted March 18, 1820 in Murphree's Valley on land donated by Daniel Murphree. The charter members were Murphrees and Bynums with few exceptions. The church moved to Friday's Crossing when land was donated by John B. Allgood and wife, in June 1892. The Mt. Moriah Cemetery preceded the arrival of the Mt. Moriah Church at that location. The first person to be buried in Mt. Moriah Cemetery was Alice Moore, the daughter of Dr. Jimmy Moore and his first wife Leila McDonald Moore. Alice died as a young child in 1885. Dr. Moore was of the Primitive Baptist faith as were a number of the Moore family.

Mt. Pleasant Baptist Church
Photo by Max Pate, 2012

Mt. Pleasant Baptist Church was organized on July 3 1859, with only ten charter members. They were Moses Ray and wife; Samuel R Reese and wife; Jacob McDonald and wife, Macinda; Samuel Brown and wife; John McNeal; and Martha McDonald. These members had withdrawn from Harmony Baptist Church to constitute Mt. Pleasant (located on a mountain near Moses Ray's home. Elder James Fields preached the first sermon and ordained members of Harmony Baptist to help organize the new church. Mt Pleasant was started primarily as a mission church for the convenience of the members in the area. The first Mt. Pleasant Church was a one-room log building located near the Mt. Moriah Cemetery.

The second building for Mt. Pleasant was built in 1864 near the present location and it, too was a one room log structure. The third building was positioned more closely to the home of

Robert C. Moore, youngest son of Dr. Jimmy Moore, still standing today. The third church was built in 1871 and was bigger than the earlier churches; however, it was still a log cabin.

In 1877, J. P. Arnold and wife donated two acres of land for the present church site. Since that time there have been three church buildings at this site. I (Max) remember working on a new church building in the 1950s. George Sloman was the foreman of the construction of this building. He had worked on the Moore farm and was a great carpenter, as well as a deacon of our church. Mt. Pleasant had been used for school classrooms when the Susan Moore schools burned in the late 1920s and again in the 1930s. It was conveniently located near to the school grounds at that time and remains on the same site today in 2012.

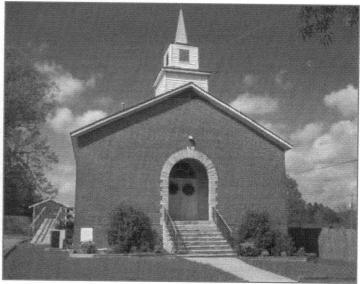

Ebenezer Methodist Church
Photo by Max Pate, 2012

Ebenezer Methodist Church was organized before 1880. W. A. Ballard and his wife gave the land for the site where the present Church building now stands. Aunt Addie Jackson was quoted in an earlier document that the first church was located west of the present building. The second building was built in 1891 just south of the present church building facing east. The Ebenezer Church belonged to the Birmingham District, Alabama Conference of the Methodist Episcopal Church. James S. Lamb was one of the first trustees of this church. The Methodist Church at Clarence joined with Ebenezer and resolved to consolidate and thereby be a stronger congregation. The meeting place was to be at Ebenezer. This resolution took place on March 23, 1955. The Susan Moore Methodist Church at Clarence Alabama was sold to Susan Moore School and the church building was used as a music room and additional classrooms when needed. The Susan Moore Methodist Church stood a little southwest of where today's Susan Moore Band Room is located.

Mt. Zion Church of God on Highway 75
Photo by Max Pate, 2012

The first church services for a Church of God in this area were held in the home of Mr. and Mrs. W. H. Ridgeway. Other attendees as given in earlier histories were Addie Ridgeway Jackson, Lois Ridgeway Jackson, Hettie Painter, Georgia Ridgeway, Lizzie Ridgeway, Georgia Laughlin, Mary Wright, Wiley Ridgeway, Herman Laughlin, Mollie Laughlin, and Eliza Peoples. In 1917, a church was built on land donated by Tom and Hettie Painter. This land was near Whippoorwill Creek, one-half mile downstream from the bridge on Highway 75. Having used the 1917 one room church for more than 20 years, in 1949, Ersie Huffstutler and his wife donated land on Highway 75 where the present (2012) Mt. Zion Church is located. T R. Jackson and his wife were instrumental in the building of this church and later donated property for future expansion and more educational facilities to be built.

**Originally Pleasant Hill Methodist Church
Currently Wynnville Community Church**

Wynnville Cemetery

Wynnville Church (Pleasant Hill) had a very important role for the community of Susan Moore in the earlier days of the development of the community of Clarence and Susan Moore. There were many singings and dinners on the ground there and also Box suppers. The young women would prepare a picnic meal for two and the young men would buy the box and eat the picnic meal with the one who had prepared it. I have a postcard from around 1910 before my grandparents were married. My grandmother was hinting to my grandfather that he should come and buy her box! Some things never change!

Chapter 15

Susan Moore High School and Community Memorabilia

Miscellaneous memorabilia from the early days of Clarence Community School to the present day Susan Moore High School in 2012 are collected here. Most of these pictures are from the collection of the C. Claude Moore family or collected from other family and community members as noted.

**Rebecca Moore, Ruby Doyle, Mary Lee Dempsey, Ivaleen Moore, Pluma Barnes, and
Malzie Green - Clarence Community School 1919**

W. A. Moore was the first principal of Susan Moore School established in 1925. He succeeded in having Susan Moore High School accredited in 1928. With construction complete in 1925, students were working diligently to graduate from the new Susan Moore High School. Four students had begun working toward a high school diploma before the completion of the first building. However, in the spring of 1928 that first building was destroyed by fire. Classes continued in the local church and in the Masonic Hall enabling those four to graduate in 1928. They were Clara Burns, Annie Lewis, Etoile Moore, and Mary Wright.

Susan Moore School students in about 1926 or 1927

Home Economics class of 1926-27
Rebecca Moore Miller on the far right, and next to her, Ivaleen Moore Currey

The first graduating class to have completed all four years of their high school days in the accredited high school was in 1929, four years after it became Susan Moore High School.

The following is a photocopy of the actual invitation for that year from the C. Claude Moore family collection.

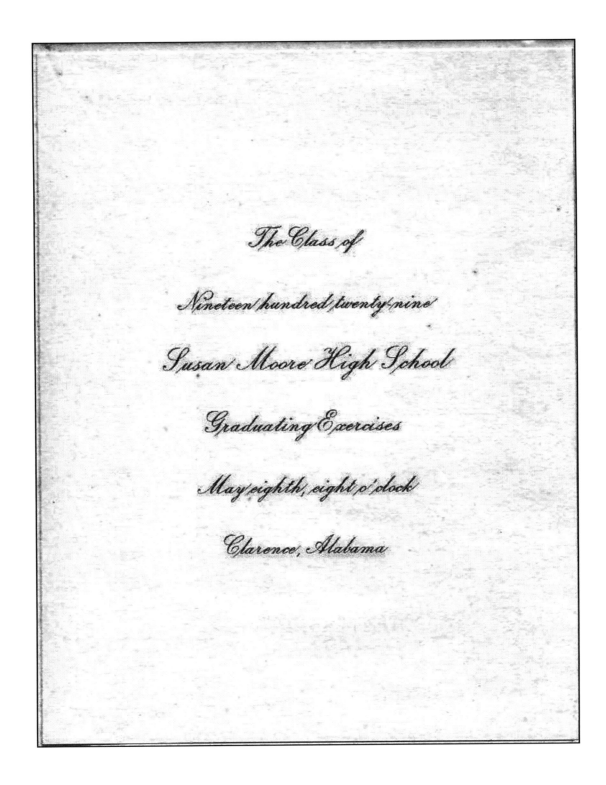

The Class of

Nineteen hundred twenty-nine

Susan Moore High School

Graduating Exercises

May eighth, eight o'clock

Clarence, Alabama

CLASS MOTTO

Climb though the rocks be rugged

CLASS COLORS

Green and White

CLASS FLOWER

White Rose

CLASS ROLL

CONSTANCE IVALEEN MOORE	ALENE MILLER
VERDIE MILLER	J. JOSEPH PAINTER
JAMIE W. FREEMAN	MAEVIS ETOILE STEPHENS
LOIS IRENE PARRISH	ILA BEATRICE DOYLE
PRUDENCE R. HORTON	ELLIS DEAN
WILLIAM C. ROBINSON	FLORA CLEVELAND
SADIE BELLE WRIGHT	PAUL S. JONES

The members of that 1929 graduation class, (graduation exercises were on May 8th at 8:00 PM), were Constance Ivaleen Moore (Valedictorian) Verdie Miller, Jamie W. Freeman, Lois Irene Parish, Prudence R. Horton, William C. Robinson, Sadie Belle Wright, Alene Miller, J. Joseph Painter, Mavis Etoile Stephens, Ila Beatrice Doyle, Ellis Dean, Flora Cleveland, and Paul S. Jones.

Susan Moore Basketball Team

Front Left to Right: William Robertson, Odell Thompson and Gordon Gibbs.
Back Left to Right: Henley Dempsey, Cordell Harvey, Joseph Painter,
Hobert Gibbs, Bernard Horton and Coach Roberts

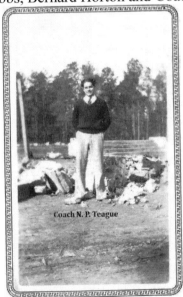

Coach N. P. Teague

The First and Second SMS Basketball Teams

Susan Moore School Football Team

Susan Moore Class of 1929

Susan Moore High School Faculty

Susan Moore High School Students

Susan Moore High School

The first brick building burned in about1936 as the original building had in the spring of 1928. The foundation of the building was salvaged and the building was rebuilt on the same foundation.

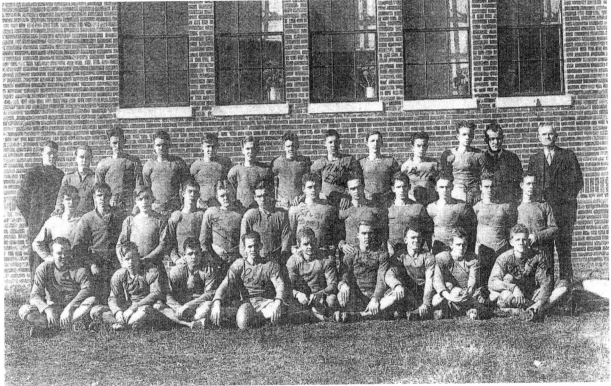

Susan Moore High School Football Team (early 30's)

1st row: Pud Morton, Roscoe Brown, Odis Lyles, Ross Debter, Spoony Baker, Cotton Long, Stuffy Stewart, Sam Wallace, Kilburn Elrod.
2nd row: Wallace McCray, Cat Hair Bowers, Odell Hudson, Dink Wallace, Willard Hanson, Arvil Hudson, Stump Long, Bert Copeland, Howard Kemp, Byron York, Aubrey Phillips, Tresie

Harvey.

3rd row: Manager – Dwight NeSmith, Roy Kimberly, Verbon Eason, Lovice Weston, Theo Jenkins, Emory C. Nash, Dude Kimberly, Mutt Elrod, Eldridge Ridgeway, Preacher Ballew, Ray Hudson, coach – Lee Roberts, principal – W. A. "Gus" Moore.

1933-34 FOOTBALL RESULTS	
Susan Moore	47
Walnut Grove	0
Susan Moore	36
Elkmont	0
Susan Moore	46
Oak Grove	0
Susan Moore	27
Blountsville	7
Susan Moore	18
Oneonta	0
Susan Moore	39
Altoona	0
Susan Moore	43
Pell City	0
Susan Moore	12
Howard College Freshmen	13

1935 county football champions

County football champions in 1935 were these Susan Moore High School students: front row, left to right, O. T. Bailey, Howard (Windy) Kemp, Webb Horton, Hobert Gregory, Cordell (Buck) Hood, Royce Bynum; second row, Onus Beasley, Clark Miller, Byron York, Jimmy Tuck, Ethridge Ridgeway, Noval Bynum; third row, Coach Wheeler (Red) Garrett, Waltene Jackson, Howard Holland, Robert Nolan, Ralph Gibbs, Kilburn Elrod, Haskel Lumpkin, Eldridge Ridgeway, Harlon Barwick, and Principal W. A. Moore.

My Aunt Ethel Moore Oden graduated in 1938. A copy of her graduation invitation is included in this memorabilia.

Class Officers

LILLIAN BALLEW - President
C. L. MILLER - Vice President
Ethel Moore - Secretary
Nancy Gill - Treasurer

CLASS MOTTO:
"Preparation is the Keynote of Success"

CLASS COLORS: Pink and Blue

CLASS FLOWER: White Rose

Class Roll

Wade Braswell	Velva Adams
M. C. Cooper	Loucile Allison
Eugene Gilliland	Elvie Bailey
David Greene	Gertie Bailey
Hobert Gregory	Lillian Ballew
Hubert Kirby	Erna Barwick
Haskell Lumpkin	Lottie Lou Bentley
Ralph Gibbs	Merle Burns
Waltene Jackson	Imalene Cuzzort
C. L. Miller	Marcell Eller
Cecil Morris	Janell Elrod
Boyd Owen	Clara Freeman
Paul Ratliff	Cleo Freeman
Jimmie Tuck	Flora French
Mary Willie French	Ethel Moore
Nancy Gill	Olinette Murphree
Venell Graham	Joree Scruggs
Elva Jenkins	Anne Margaret Tuck
Imogene Kerr	Gertrude Bryant Tuck
Margaret Lamb	Earnesteen Young
Florence Lindsay	

The Senior Class

Susan Moore High School

Graduation Exercises

Monday Evening, May Ninth

eight o'clock

Susan Moore High School 1958

Susan Moore High School 1960's

Susan Moore Elementary School
Photo by Max Pate, 2012

Chapter 16

The Town of Susan Moore

The Moore families were pioneers to the Eastern section of northeast Blount County. The contributions of this family and the respect for a mother, Susan Nunnalley Moore, the wife of Dr. David S. Moore and the mother of the medical doctors, Dr. D.S. Moore, Jr. and Dr. Joe G.. Moore who financed the building of the first Susan Moore High School led to the naming of the community as Susan Moore and officially naming the town Susan Moore. The town was incorporated as Susan Moore in 1982. An election on December 21, 1981 named T. R. Jackson as Mayor and the following individuals were elected to serve as council members: J. L. "Lou" Painter, Joel M. Ballard, J. Malton Jackson, Robbie Bryan, and W. F. Bill Smallwood. Several people have served as Mayor between the first Mayor T. R. Jackson and the present Mayor James B. Brothers. The only woman having served as Mayor to date was Mayor Lillian Leathers. The town officials and the local Fire Department members have been assets to the area, laboring hard and long at whatever the need. Many people have contributed to the development of this town over the years. There are other things that have not yet been mentioned which contributed to the early development of the town, my husband, Jerry R. Jackson worked with Mayor T. R. Jackson to develop the first police department of the town. As Jerry was already a graduate of Northeast Alabama Law Enforcement Academy at Jacksonville State University and had experience being a Chief of Police, he became Susan Moore's first Chief of Police. Jerry was a full time teacher so after the department was organized, he decided to follow his career in education and give up the part time work he was contributing. Assistant Chief Tim Kent, also part time, continued to serve the town. Later, there were several people who worked in Susan Moore's police department. The town members as much as the school students have always had much love for their school, their athletic programs, their "Bulldogs" and their memories of by-gone days. The statewide celebration called The Great Alabama Homecoming in 2010 was part of the Year of Alabama small Towns and Downtowns. It was designed to celebrate "everything" that is Sweet Home Alabama. Those of us who have lived here, gone to school here, cheered our Bulldogs on toward victory know that "Susan Moore" is indeed Sweet Home Alabama!

When 215 small towns designed their celebrations, this event was the impetus for Susan

Moore's small town celebration on June 19, 2010. What a day of sharing of old pictures, old memories and recognition of the Moore Family and others who helped to make this area what it is and has been through the years. The people of Susan Moore have always been hardworking dedicated people who are proud of their school and its achievements and proud of the town of Susan Moore.

The following article was taken from the Blount Countian, a local hometown newspaper:

The Blount Countian • Section B • June 30, 2010

Susan Moore celebration

by Wallace Todd

In 1864, Dr. Robert M. Moore left his home in Georgia, traveling alone in an oxcart. While passing through northern Blount County, he was awed by the beauty of the area and its fertile soil. He entered an entire section of land and returned to Georgia.

After persuading his wife to move to the new haven he had found in Alabama, he loaded her and 10 children into a covered wagon and headed west to settle on his section of land.

David, one of Dr. Moore's sons, became a doctor and married Susan Nunnally. As his children married, he gave each a parcel of land. Around 1883, Dr. David Moore named the place of his first home Clarence, in honor of his first-born son.

When their mother Susan died in 1923, brothers David and Joe, also a physician, constructed a school and named it after their mother.

By 1960, some Clarence residents felt that the neighboring town of Snead was eyeing the school and community with intent to annex them. To defend their school, residents met in November 1982 and decided they should establish their own town.

At an election held Dec. 21 that year, T. R. Jackson was named mayor and J. L. Painter, J. M. Ballard, J. M. Jackson, Robbie Bryan, and W. F. Smallwood were elected council members. The town was incorporated as Susan Moore. Some Moore descendants still reside in the area.

Now Susan Moore is a town of more than 900 residents on about 3000 acres in northern Blount County. It is a community of proud, hard-working people whose daily lives are not much different from any others'.

But June 19 was special.

A standing-room-only crowd filled the town hall to join in the statewide celebra-

See CELEBRATION,
continued to page 3 of this section

Sharing festivities at Susan Moore's celebration are councilmen (from left) J.J. Brothers, Jeff Russell, and Bobby Waddle, along with Mayor Jamie Brothers, Gary McGill, Sheriff Loyd Arrington, Rep. Elwyn Thomas, and Probate Judge David Standridge. Councilmen Randal Gilliland and Gerald Richardson are not pictured.

THE BLOUNT COUNTIAN / SECTION B / ONEONTA, ALABAMA / JUNE 30, 2010 / PAGE 3

CELEBRATION

CONTINUED FROM SECTION FRONT

tion of "Alabama Small Towns and Downtowns." Mayor Jamie Brothers began the festivities by recognizing some of the town's founders and volunteer workers. "Without these people, there would not be a town of Susan Moore," the mayor said.

In addition to town officials, several other elected officials took part in the celebration, including state Rep. Elwyn Thomas, Probate Judge David Standridge, Sheriff Loyd Arrington, and Oneonta Mayor Darryl Ray, former Susan Moore resident. Thomas surprised the mayor with a $5000 check to further upgrade and beautify the town's public facilities.

A dedication ceremony took place at an impressive welcoming area that had been completed on the grounds in time for the festivities. U.S., Alabama, and Susan Moore flags flew proudly, and special recognition was given the mayor and the town's first clerk, Lucille Adams Holmes. Centering the area is a handsome marker, a gift of the state tourism department. Elsewhere on the grounds three simple stone monu-

ments list the names of town leaders, donors, and businesses.

A ladies auxiliary headed by town clerk Beverly Mize provided plenty of food and drinks for the crowd, and a local vendor offered barbecue and catfish plates, but a downpour of rain had interrupted activities and few celebrators remained for the generous meal. Some entertainment had been presented, and visitors were

offered a tour of Robbie Bryan's nearby museum.

Visible everywhere was landscaping that beautified the area around the town hall, bridges having been built over the creek, whose bank was covered with blooming day lilies.

Clarence/Susan Moore community has come a long way since Dr. Moore rode in from Georgia on his oxcart, and it's still moving forward with pride.

Memorials at the Susan Moore Town Hall

TOWN OF SUSAN MOORE

In 1864, traveling in an ox cart. Mr. Robert M. Moore left his family in Walton County, Georgia, and journeyed to Blount County, Alabama. Finding fertile land, he returned to Walton County and persuaded his wife to move to Blount County with him. In 1865, his wife and 10 children: William T., Zachariah C., Robert B., David S., B. Martin, John M., Jimmy H., D. Marion, Nancy C., and Sally, traveled in a covered wagon and settled in Moore's section of land. All of the children married. As each child married, he or she was given a tract of land. David married Susan Nunnally. In 1883, Mr. Moore named the community where he built his first house, Clarence, in honor of his oldest son. Mr. Moore's office and drugstore were located in his home. His sons, David Jr., and Joe both became medical doctors. They and another doctor became partners and founded South Highland Hospital in Birmingham. In 1923, when Susan Moore died, David Moore Jr., and Joe were moved at their mother's funeral to donate monies for the construction of a consolidated school in her honor. Susan Moore School was named. Robert B. Moore's oldest son, William Augustus was the first principal of Susan Moore High School.
(Continued on other side)

ERECTED BY THE ALABAMA TOURISM DEPARTMENT AND THE TOWN OF SUSAN MOORE
JUNE 2010

TOWN OF SUSAN MOORE

(Continued from other side)

The other sons became successful farmers and the daughters married farmers. Many descendants still live in this area and have made civic contributions to the community in many ways. Through the early years, farming was the main occupation of the residents. Corn and cotton were the money crops. The community of Clarence had a gin, sawmill and a sorghum mill. Grocery stores were owned by various families throughout the community. On November 18, 1982, the residents of the community of Clarence decided to hold an election. The following month on December 21, an election was held to elect the council. Elected to the first council were J. L. Painter, J. M. Ballard, J. M. Jackson, R. F. Bryan and W. F. Smallwood. The council members elected T. R. Jackson as mayor. The council voted on naming the town Susan Moore. The town was incorporated with 960 acres and a population of 351. The first clerk was Lucille Holmes.

ERECTED BY THE ALABAMA TOURISM DEPARTMENT AND THE TOWN OF SUSAN MOORE
JUNE 2010

Current map of Susan Moore

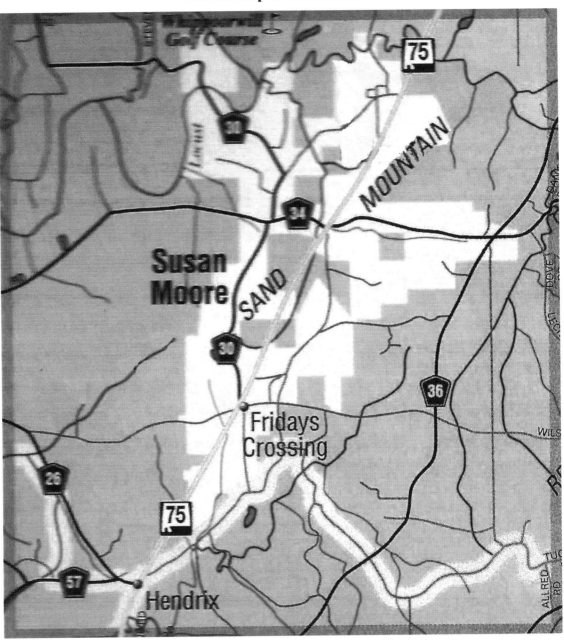

REFERENCES

Blount County Heritage Committee (1999). The heritage of Blount County, Alabama, Vol 5. 2nd printing. Heritage Publishing Consultants, Inc. Clanton, Alabama.

Blount County Historical Society (1977). The heritage of Blount County. Bicentennial Edition. Taylor Publishing Company.

Bryan, R. & Jenkins, P. (2009). *Out the road and around the corner with an occasional glance in the rear view mirror.* Blount Office Supply, Publisher.

Burns, Jesse (1923). *Great day at Uncle Zack Moore's. The Southern Democrat.* Obtained from Susan Moore 1865-1989: Reunion Committee.

Catalog of the Officers and students of the University of Alabama (1901-1902). Tuscaloosa: University of Alabama.

Final Services for David S. Moore. (1947 June 10). The Birmingham News. Birmingham, AL.

Hatley, G. (1923). *Mrs. Susan Moore, an obituary. The Southern Democrat.* Reprinted from Death Notices from the Southern Democrat 1920-1927. P. 118.

Holley, H. (1982). *The History of Medicine in Alabama.* University of Alabama School of Medicine. Birmingham, AL.

In ill health for many years – Dr Joseph G. Moore, 65, widely know doctor, dies, (1954, July 21). Birmingham News, Birmingham, AL.

Moore, R. C. & Moore, L. O. (1973). The Family Tree of Robert M. Moore. Unpublished

Moore, C T (1903). Geological Relation of the Deposits of Hematite and Limonite in the Birmingham District of Alabama, 1902.

Obituary of Grady L. Phillips retrieved on Mar 4 2012 from Roots Web Listserve.

    Message Board URL: http://boards.rootsweb.com/topics.obits2/9660/mb.ashx

Obituary for Dr. David S. Moore, Sr. (1932, Dec 10) Birmingham News,

    Birmingham, AL.

Obituary of Dr. D. S, Moore, Jr. (1947, June 12) The Southern Democrat.

Obituary of Mrs. Susan Moore, A Pioneer Blount Countian, (1923 Mar 11) The Southern

    Democrat.

Owens, T. M. & Owens, M. B. (1921) History of Alabama and Dictionary of Alabama

Biography, Vol. IV. Chicago: S. J. Clarke Publishing.

Prominent Citizen Dies. (1939). The Southern Democrat. Blount County, AL.

Register of University of Alabama Students (190l) Tuscaloosa: University of Alabama.

Susan Moore Reunion Committee (1989). Susan Moore 1865-1989. Susan Moore, Blount

    County, AL.

United States Federal Census Records. 1790 – 1930.

University of Alabama Catalog (1902) Tuscaloosa, AL: University of Alabama.

The Moore Family Genealogy

Prof. Claude Moore and daughter, Ivaleen.

Descendants of Zachariah Moore

Generation 1

1   **ZACHARIAH**[1] **MOORE** was born on 10 Dec 1799 in Newberry, South Carolina, United States. He died on 16 Dec 1860 in Monroe, Walton County, Georgia USA. He married **MARY STILL** on 25 Dec 1823 in Walton, Georgia, United States. She was born on 08 Dec 1802 in Edgefield, Edgefield, South Carolina, United States. She died on 27 Sep 1880 in Monroe, Walton, Georgia, USA (Burial in Moore Cemetery, Walton, GA).

Zachariah Moore and Mary Still had the following children:

106.   i.   NANCY SIDNEY[2] MOORE (daughter of Zachariah Moore and Mary Still) was born on
    ii. Dec 1824 in Walton, Georgia, United States. She died on 10 Apr 1906 in Italy, Ellis, Texas, United States (Monument in Italy Cemetery). She married WILLIAM L. BILLY MORGAN.

3.   ii. ROBERT MARIAN MOORE (son of Zachariah Moore and Mary Still) was born on 13 Dec 1825 in Walton, Georgia, United States. He died on 20 Sep 1877 in Blountsville, Blount, Alabama, United States (Burial in Salem Primitive Baptist Cemetery ar Brooksville). He married NANCY JANE WATSON on 28 Dec 1846 in Walton Co. GA USA (Marriage). She was born on 04 Jan 1827 in Walton, Georgia, United States. She died on 24 Nov 1910 in Blountsville, Blount, Alabama, United States.

4.   iii. ELIZABETH JANE "BETSY" MOORE (daughter of Zachariah Moore and Mary Still) was born on 03 Jun 1827 in Walton, Georgia, United States. She died on 04 Mar 1885 in Walton, Georgia, United States. She married ELISHA BENNETT WATSON on 03 Dec 1848 in Walton, Georgia, United States. He was born on 02 Jul 1829 in Loganville, Walton, Georgia, United States. He died on 20 May 1903 in Barry, Navarro, Texas, United States.

5.   iv. WILLIAM YOUNG MOORE (son of Zachariah Moore and Mary Still) was born on 11 Jun 1829 in Walton, Georgia, United States. He died on 24 Jan 1880 in Walton, Georgia, United States. He married (1) FRANCES MATILDA EDWARDS on 17 Nov 1872. She was born on 15 Oct 1843 in Georgia, United States. She died on 12 May 1916 in Georgia, United States. He married (2) SARAH SIMONTON on 13 Oct 1843 in Walton, Georgia, United States. She was born on 27 Mar 1834 in Walton, Georgia, United States. She died on 29 Aug 1870 in Walton, Georgia, United States.

    v. SALLY M MOORE (daughter of Zachariah Moore and Mary Still) was born on 28 Sep 1831 in Walton, Georgia, United States. She died on 28 Sep 1839 in Walton, Georgia, United States.

6.   vi. BENJAMIN STILL MOORE (son of Zachariah Moore and Mary Still) was born on 17 Nov 1833 in Walton, Georgia, United States. He died on 11 Dec 1906 in Walton, Georgia, United States. He married MARTHA MATILDA BULLOCK on 02 Dec 1855 in Walton, Georgia, United States. She was born on 06 Jan 1835 in Walton, Georgia, United States. She died on 02 Mar 1894 in Walton, Georgia, United States.

7.   vii. SARAH ANN MOORE (daughter of Zachariah Moore and Mary Still) was born on 30 Dec 1835 in Walton, Georgia, United States. She died on 31 May 1907 in Walton, Georgia, United States (Shiloh Cem. Walton Co. GA). She married JAMES M. HEAD on 07 Apr 1878 in Walton Co., GA. He was born on 11 Sep 1829 in Elbert County, Georgia, USA. He died on 09 May 1910 in Gwinnett, Georgia, USA.

viii. MARTHA E. MOORE (daughter of Zachariah Moore and Mary Still) was born on 31 Dec 1837 in Walton, Georgia, United States. She died on 24 Aug 1920 in Walton, Georgia, United States (Towler Cemetery). She married DAVID GANAWAY DURDEN on 18 May 1890 in Book, Uecker-Randow, Mecklenburg-Vorpommern, Germany, son of Elisha Durden and Martha Nancy Conner. He was born on 06 Apr 1826 in Walton, Georgia, United States. He died on 21 Apr 1902 in Buried Towler Cemetery, Walton, Georgia, United States.

8. ix. DAVID MARTIN MOORE (son of Zachariah Moore and Mary Still) was born on 08 Apr 1842 in Walton, Georgia, United States. He died on 14 Apr 1878 in Walton, Georgia, United States. He married MARTHA MATILDA SMITH. She was born on 02 an 1847 in Walton Co. GA USA. She died on 12 Mar 1877 in Walton Co. GA USA.

9. x. THOMAS JEFFERSON MOORE (son of Zachariah Moore and Mary Still) was born on 24 Nov 1844 in Walton, Georgia, United States. He died on 02 Jan 1927 in Ennis, Ellis, Texas, United States. He married (1) LAURA JOSEPHINE CRAMER on 22 Nov 1874 in Walton, Georgia, United States. She was born on 02 Feb 1856 in Georgia, United States. She died on 18 Jun 1924 in Ellis, Texas, United States. He married (2) FRANCES PERMELIA SMITH on 14 Nov 1867 in Walton, Georgia, United States. She was born on 11 Jan 1851 in Walton, Georgia, United States. She died on 17 Mar 1874 in Walton, Georgia, United States.

Generation 2

2. NANCY SIDNEY^2 MOORE (Zachariah^1) was born on 08 Dec 1824 in Walton, Georgia, United States. She died on 10 Apr 1906 in Italy, Ellis, Texas, United States (Monument in Italy Cemetery). She married WILLIAM L. BILLY MORGAN.

William L. Billy Morgan and Nancy Sidney Moore had the following children:

i. JOSHUA ALBERT^3 MORGAN (son of William L. Billy Morgan and Nancy Sidney Moore) was born on 03 Jul 1846 in Walton Co., GA.

ii. MARY JANE MORGAN (daughter of William L. Billy Morgan and Nancy Sidney Moore) was born on 30 Oct 1847 in Walton Co., GA. She died on 26 Nov 1886 in Ellis, Texas, United States.

iii. FRANCISE ELIZABETH MORGAN (daughter of William L. Billy Morgan and Nancy Sidney Moore) was born on 16 Mar 1849 in Walton Co., GA. She died on 21 Sep 1933 in Italy, Ellis, Texas, United States.

iv. JOHN WILSON MORGAN (son of William L. Billy Morgan and Nancy Sidney Moore) was born on 07 Nov 1850 in Walton Co., GA. He died in Italy, Ellis Co., Texas.

v. MARTHA A. C. MORGAN (daughter of William L. Billy Morgan and Nancy Sidney Moore) was born on 15 Sep 1852 in Walton Co., GA. She died on 15 Apr 1878.

vi. ZACHARIAH M. MORGAN (son of William L. Billy Morgan and Nancy Sidney Moore) was born on 25 Feb 1855 in Ellis Co., TX. He died on 25 Jul 1863 in Slay, Texas, United States.

vii. NANCY JANE MORGAN (daughter of William L. Billy Morgan and Nancy Sidney Moore) was born on 07 Jan 1857 in Ellis Co., TX. She died on 06 Aug 1886 in TX.

viii. RACHEL MORGAN (daughter of William L. Billy Morgan and Nancy Sidney Moore) was born on 03 Mar 1860 in Ellis Co., TX. She died on 01 Apr 1927 in Ellis, Texas, United States.

3.   **ROBERT MARIAN**[2] **MOORE** (Zachariah[1]) was born on 13 Dec 1825 in Walton, Georgia, United States. He died on 20 Sep 1877 in Blountsville, Blount, Alabama, United States (Burial in Salem Primitive Baptist Cemetery ar Brooksville). He married **NANCY JANE WATSON** on 28 Dec 1846 in Walton Co. GA USA (Marriage). She was born on 04 Jan 1827 in Walton, Georgia, United States. She died on 24 Nov 1910 in Blountsville, Blount, Alabama, United States.

Robert Marian Moore and Nancy Jane Watson had the following children:

      i.   WILLIAM T.[3] MOORE (son of Robert Marian Moore and Nancy Jane Watson) was born on 10 Dec 1847 in Walton, Georgia, USA. He died in 1865 in Tennessee, USA.

10.   ii.   ZACHARIAH E MOORE (son of Robert Marian Moore and Nancy Jane Watson) was born on 20 Feb 1849 in Walton, Georgia, USA. He died on 21 Jul 1924 in Blount, Alabama, USA (Burial in Wynnville Cem.). He married JOSEPHINE P. NUNNALLY. She was born on 11 Sep 1849 in Walton, Georgia, United States. She died on 24 Mar 1934 in Blount Co., Ala (Burial in Wynnville Cem.).

11.   iii.   ROBERT BENNETT MOORE I (son of Robert Marian Moore and Nancy Jane Watson) was born on 16 Oct 1850 in Walton, Georgia, USA. He died on 03 Sep 1901 in Blount, Alabama, USA (Burial in Mt. Moriah Cemetery). He married SARAH ELIZABETH HICKS on 21 Nov 1872 in Blount, Alabama. She was born on 21 Oct 1853 in Alabama, United States. She died on 13 Jun 1931 in Blount, Alabama, United States (Burial in Mt. Moriah Cem).

12.   iv.   DAVID SANDERS MOORE MD (son of Robert Marian Moore and Nancy Jane Watson) was born on 19 Mar 1852 in Near Lawrenceville, Walton County, GA. He died on 09 Dec 1932 in Blount, Alabama, USA (Wynnville Cem. Blount Co., AL). He married SUSAN ALEXANDRIA NUNNALLEY on 25 Mar 1875 in Blount, Alabama. She was born on 25 Sep 1854 in Georgia. She died on 01 Mar 1923 in Blount, Alabama, United States (Burial in Wynnville Cem.).

13.   v.   BENJAMIN MARTIN MOORE (son of Robert Marian Moore and Nancy Jane Watson) was born on 23 Mar 1854 in Walton Co. GA USA. He died on 25 Feb 1943 in Blount Co.Alabama, USA (Burial in Mt. Moriah Cemetery). He married HAVANNA FANNIE SCRUGGS. She was born on 07 Mar 1860 in Alabama, United States. She died on 19 Jan 1926 in Clarence, Blount, Alabama.

14.   vi.   JOHN MORGAN MOORE (son of Robert Marian Moore and Nancy Jane Watson) was born on 17 Sep 1855 in Monroe, Walton, Georgia. He died on 01 Aug 1935 in Blount, Alabama, USA (Burial in Mt. Moriah Cem). He married (1) FANNIE COX, daughter of Albert Ewing Cox and Juliet Warren Alford. She was born in 1859 in Georgia, United States. He married (2) EMMA ENTREKIN in Blount, Alabama. She was born in May 1870 in Georgia, United States. He married (3) SUSAN MILLIE GRIFFIN. She was born in Aug 1876 in , , Alabama, USA.

15.   vii.   DR. JAMES "JIMMY" HAMILTON MOORE D.MD (son of Robert Marian Moore and Nancy Jane Watson) was born on 08 Mar 1858 in Walton, Georgia, USA. He died on 27 Mar 1939 in Blount, Alabama, USA (Burial in Mt. Moriah Cem). He married (1) LEILA ISADORE MCDONALD on 17 Feb 1881 in Blount County, Alabama, USA (Burial in Mt. Moriah Cemetery). She was born on 03 Dec 1864 in Alabama. She died on 18 Mar 1886 in Blount, AL, USA (Burial in Mt. Moriah Cemetery). He married (2) ELEANOR E RAY in 1888 in Blount, Alabama, United States (Burial in Mt. Moriah Cemetery), daughter of Moses (Maso) Ray and Elizabeth McDonald. She was born on 04 Nov 1869 in Alabama, United States. She died on 22 May 1890 in Blount, Alabama, United States (Burial in Mt. Moriah Cemetery). He married (3) SAVANNAH VILULA BYNUM in 1890 in Blount, Alabama, United States (Burial in Mt. Moriah Cemetery). She was born on 03 Dec 1870 in Blount, Alabama, United States. She died on 16 Apr 1939 in Blount, Alabama, United States (Burial in Mt. Moriah Cemetery).

16. viii. DANIEL MARION MOORE (son of Robert Marian Moore and Nancy Jane Watson) was born on 13 Aug 1859 in Walton, Georgia, USA. He died on 08 Sep 1942 in Blount, Alabama, USA. He married MARIE OLGA MALZIE GREEN on 25 Feb 1883 in Blount, Alabama, USA. She was born on 18 Jun 1867 in Alabama, USA. She died on 22 Jun 1943 in Mon... Pt., Shelby, Alabama.

17. ix. NANCY A ELIZABETH MOORE (daughter of Robert Marian Moore and Nancy Jane Watson) was born on 13 Aug 1861 in Walton, Georgia, USA. She died on 22 Jun 1891 in Blount, Alabama, USA. She married JOHN QUINCY ADAMS on 17 Jul 1881 in Blount, Alabama, United States, son of Elijah Adams and Orenna Brown. He was born on 11 Nov 1858 in Dale, Alabama, United States. He died on 07 Sep 1919 in Blount, Alabama, United States.

18. x. EMMA JANE MARY MOORE (daughter of Robert Marian Moore and Nancy Jane Watson) was born on 08 Aug 1864 in Georgia, United States. She died on 12 Nov 1912 in Blount, Alabama, USA. She married ASBERRY NEWTON BUD BALLARD. He was born on 19 Mar 1861 in Mississippi, United States. He died on 05 Jun 1948.

4. ELIZABETH JANE "BETSY"[2] MOORE (Zachariah[1]) was born on 03 Jun 1827 in Walton, Georgia, United States. She died on 04 Mar 1885 in Walton, Georgia, United States. She married ELISHA BENNETT WATSON on 03 Dec 1848 in Walton, Georgia, United States. He was born on 02 Jul 1829 in Loganville, Walton, Georgia, United States. He died on 20 May 1903 in Barry, Navarro, Texas, United States.

Elisha Bennett Watson and Elizabeth Jane "Betsy" Moore had the following children:

i. JAMES ROBERT[3] WATSON (son of Elisha Bennett Watson and Elizabeth Jane "Betsy" Moore) was born on 28 Oct 1849 in Walton, Georgia, United States. He died on 09 Jul 1931 in Corsicana, Navarro, Texas, United States.

ii. MARY A WATSON (daughter of Elisha Bennett Watson and Elizabeth Jane "Betsy" Moore) was born on 28 Jun 1851 in Walton, Georgia, United States. She died on 05 Sep 1889 in Walton, Georgia, United States.

iii. JOHN N WATSON (son of Elisha Bennett Watson and Elizabeth Jane "Betsy" Moore) was born in 1854 in Walton, Georgia, United States. He died on 12 Jan 1941.

iv. THOMAS JEFFERSON WATSON (son of Elisha Bennett Watson and Elizabeth Jane "Betsy" Moore) was born in 1856 in Walton, Georgia, United States. He died on 20 Oct 1925 in Haskell, Haskell, Texas, United States.

v. NANCY SIDNEY WATSON (daughter of Elisha Bennett Watson and Elizabeth Jane "Betsy" Moore) was born on 30 Sep 1857 in Walton, Georgia, United States. She died on 12 Jan 1941 in Rural Shade, Navarro, Texas, United States.

vi. WILLIAM ELISHA WATSON (son of Elisha Bennett Watson and Elizabeth Jane "Betsy" Moore) was born in 1861 in Walton, Georgia, United States. He died on 21 Mar 1932.

vii. MARY ALICE WATSON (daughter of Elisha Bennett Watson and Elizabeth Jane "Betsy" Moore) was born in 1882 in Walton, Georgia, United States. She died in Georgia, United States.

5. WILLIAM YOUNG[2] MOORE (Zachariah[1]) was born on 11 Jun 1829 in Walton, Georgia, United States. He died on 24 Jan 1880 in Walton, Georgia, United States. He married (1) FRANCES MATILDA EDWARDS on 17 Nov 1872. She was born on 15 Oct 1843 in Georgia, United States. She died on 12 May 1916 in Georgia, United States. He married (2) SARAH SIMONTON on 13 Oct 1843 in Walton, Georgia, United States. She was born on 27 Mar 1834 in Walton, Georgia, United States. She died on 29 Aug 1870 in Walton, Georgia, United States.

William Young Moore and Frances Matilda Edwards had the following children:

i. NANCY JANE[3] MOORE (daughter of William Young Moore and Frances Matilda Edwards) was born on 14 Dec 1873 in Walton, Georgia, United States. She died on 12 Oct 1960 in Walton, Georgia, United States.

ii. WILLIAM DAVID MOORE (son of William Young Moore and Frances Matilda Edwards) was born on 07 Aug 1875 in Walton, Georgia, United States. He died on 04 Aug 1914.

iii. OLIVIA T MOORE (daughter of William Young Moore and Frances Matilda Edwards) was born on 11 Jan 1877 in Walton, Georgia, United States. She died on 29 May 1914 in Georgia, United States.

iv. LENORA F MOORE (daughter of William Young Moore and Frances Matilda Edwards) was born on 16 Jan 1879 in Walton, Georgia, United States. She died in Walton, Georgia, United States.

William Young Moore and Sarah Simonton had the following children:

v. SOPHRONIA MOORE (daughter of William Young Moore and Sarah Simonton) was born in Aug 1850 in Georgia, United States.

vi. GEORGIA ANN MOORE (daughter of William Young Moore and Sarah Simonton) was born on 23 Aug 1854 in Walton, Georgia, United States.

vii. JAMES R MOORE (son of William Young Moore and Sarah Simonton) was born on 22 May 1857 in Walton, Georgia, United States. He died on 19 Jul 1928 in Walton, Georgia, United States.

viii. FRANKLIN H MOORE (son of William Young Moore and Sarah Simonton) was born on 10 Aug 1859 in Walton, Georgia, United States. He died on 31 Oct 1876 in Georgia, United States.

ix. ELIZABETH MOORE (daughter of William Young Moore and Sarah Simonton) was born in 1866 in Alabama, United States.

x. STEPHEN THOMAS MOORE (son of William Young Moore and Sarah Simonton) was born on 28 Mar 1866 in Walton, Georgia, United States. He died on 21 Nov 1937 in Georgia, United States.

xi. MARY MOORE (daughter of William Young Moore and Sarah Simonton) was born on 4 Jan 1868 in Walton, Georgia, United States. She died on 29 Aug 1870.

6. **BENJAMIN STILL**[2] **MOORE** (Zachariah[1]) was born on 17 Nov 1833 in Walton, Georgia, United States. He died on 11 Dec 1906 in Walton, Georgia, United States. He married **MARTHA MATILDA BULLOCK** on 02 Dec 1855 in Walton, Georgia, United States. She was born on 06 Jan 1835 in Walton, Georgia, United States. She died on 02 Mar 1894 in Walton, Georgia, United States.

Benjamin Still Moore and Martha Matilda Bullock had the following children:

i. WILLIAM BENNETT[3] MOORE (son of Benjamin Still Moore and Martha Matilda Bullock) was born in Jun 1859 in Walton, Georgia, United States. He died in 1935 in Walton, Georgia, United States.

ii. ROBERT DAVID MOORE (son of Benjamin Still Moore and Martha Matilda Bullock) was born on 20 Jan 1861 in Walton, Georgia, United States. He died on 31 Oct 1933 in Walton, Georgia, United States.

iii. SARA FRANCES MOORE (daughter of Benjamin Still Moore and Martha Matilda Bullock) was born on 11 May 1862 in Walton, Georgia, United States. She died on 20 Jul 1912.

      iv.   MARY JANE MOORE (daughter of Benjamin Still Moore and Martha Matilda Bullock) was born on 06 Mar 1870. She died on 08 Mar 1898.

      v.   M T MOORE (son of Benjamin Still Moore and Martha Matilda Bullock) was born in 1873.

7.   SARAH ANN^2 MOORE (Zachariah^1) was born on 30 Dec 1835 in Walton, Georgia, United States. She died on 31 May 1907 in Walton, Georgia, United States (Shiloh Cem. Walton Co. GA). She married JAMES M. HEAD on 07 Apr 1878 in Walton Co., GA. He was born on 11 Sep 1829 in Elbert County, Georgia, USA. He died on 09 May 1910 in Gwinnett, Georgia, USA.

James M. Head and Sarah Ann Moore had the following children:

      i.   MERETT^3 HEAD (son of James M. Head and Sarah Ann Moore) was born about 1861 in Walton Co. GA USA.

      ii.   CHARLES HEAD (son of James M. Head and Sarah Ann Moore) was born in Mar 1866 in Georgia. He died on 29 Dec 1943 in Gwinnett, Georgia, USA.

      iii.   AMMA HEAD (daughter of James M. Head and Sarah Ann Moore) was born on 24 Jul 1871 in Georgia, USA. She died on 20 Oct 1929 in Lawrenceville, Gwinnett, Georgia, USA.

8.   DAVID MARTIN^2 MOORE (Zachariah^1) was born on 08 Apr 1842 in Walton, Georgia, United States. He died on 14 Apr 1878 in Walton, Georgia, United States. He married MARTHA MATILDA SMITH. She was born on 02 Jan 1847 in Walton Co. GA USA. She died on 12 Mar 1877 in Walton Co. GA USA.

David Martin Moore and Martha Matilda Smith had the following children:

      i.   WILLIAM ANDREW^3 MOORE (son of David Martin Moore and Martha Matilda Smith) was born on 29 Sep 1866 in Walton Co. GA USA. He died on 22 Sep 1945 in Nashville, Berrien County Georgia.

      ii.   JAMES WASHINGTON MOORE (son of David Martin Moore and Martha Matilda Smith) was born on 14 Aug 1868 in Walton Co. GA USA. He died on 19 Dec 1953 in Tifton, Tift County, Georgia.

      iii.   MARY FRANCES MOORE (daughter of David Martin Moore and Martha Matilda Smith) was born on 11 Nov 1870 in Walton County Ga. She died on 07 Jul 1927 in Barrow County, Georgia.

      iv.   SARAH EMMER MOORE (daughter of David Martin Moore and Martha Matilda Smith) was born on 23 Nov 1872 in Walton Count y Ga. She died on 07 Apr 1873 in Walton County Ga.

      v.   DAVID THOMAS MOORE (son of David Martin Moore and Martha Matilda Smith) was born on 12 Sep 1874 in Georgia. He died on 26 Sep 1953 in Tiff County, Georgia.

9.   THOMAS JEFFERSON^2 MOORE (Zachariah^1) was born on 24 Nov 1844 in Walton, Georgia, United States. He died on 02 Jan 1927 in Ennis, Ellis, Texas, United States. He married (1) LAURA JOSEPHINE CRAMER on 22 Nov 1874 in Walton, Georgia, United States. She was born on 02 Feb 1856 in Georgia, United States. She died on 18 Jun 1924 in Ellis, Texas, United States. He married (2) FRANCES PERMELIA SMITH on 14 Nov 1867 in Walton, Georgia, United States. She was born on 11 Jan 1851 in Walton, Georgia, United States. She died on 17 Mar 1874 in Walton, Georgia, United States.

Thomas Jefferson Moore and Laura Josephine Cramer had the following children:

i. ANNIE ORA[3] MOORE (daughter of Thomas Jefferson Moore and Laura Josephine Cramer) was born in 1879 in Walton, Georgia, United States. She died in Ennis, Ellis, Texas, United States.

ii. EDGAR EVAN MOORE (son of Thomas Jefferson Moore and Laura Josephine Cramer) was born in 1881 in Walton, Georgia, United States. He died in 1933 in Fort Worth, Tarrant, Texas, United States.

iii. CLYDE THOMAS MOORE (son of Thomas Jefferson Moore and Laura Josephine Cramer) was born on 19 Nov 1883 in Walton, Georgia, United States. He died on 21 Sep 1952 in Ennis, Ellis, Texas, United States.

iv. MARY M MOORE (daughter of Thomas Jefferson Moore and Laura Josephine Cramer) was born in May 1891 in Georgia.

Thomas Jefferson Moore and Frances Permelia Smith had the following children:

v. MARY FRANCES MOORE (daughter of Thomas Jefferson Moore and Frances Permelia Smith) was born in Walton, Georgia, United States.

vi. MARTHA PEARL MOORE (daughter of Thomas Jefferson Moore and Frances Permelia Smith) was born on 06 Sep 1872 in Walton, Georgia, United States. She died on 20 Jul 1901 in Bardwell, Ellis, Texas, USA.

Generation 3

10. ZACHARIAH E[3] MOORE (Robert Marian[2], Zachariah[1]) was born on 20 Feb 1849 in Walton, Georgia, USA. He died on 21 Jul 1924 in Blount, Alabama, USA (Burial in Wynnville Cem.). He married JOSEPHINE P. NUNNALLY. She was born on 11 Sep 1849 in Walton, Georgia, United States. She died on 24 Mar 1934 in Blount Co., Ala (Burial in Wynnville Cem.).

Zachariah E Moore and Josephine P. Nunnally had the following children:

i. NANCY CAROLINE[4] MOORE (daughter of Zachariah E Moore and Josephine P. Nunnally) was born on 22 Sep 1871 in Blount Co., Alabama.. She died on 28 Feb 1882 in Susan Moore, Alabama (buried in Wynnville Cemetery).

ii. JAMES THOMAS MOORE (son of Zachariah E Moore and Josephine P. Nunnally) was born on 20 Jun 1880 in Alabama. He died on 07 Oct 1882 in Susan Moore, Alabama (Burial in Wynnville Cem.).

iii. INZER ALEXANDER MOORE (son of Zachariah E Moore and Josephine P. Nunnally) was born on 11 Aug 1883 in Alabama. He died on 09 Jan 1900 in Susan Moore, Alabama (Wynnville Cem. Blount Co., AL).

iv. IDA VESTA MOORE (daughter of Zachariah E Moore and Josephine P. Nunnally) was born on 30 Jan 1885 in Alabama. She died on 05 Oct 1964 in Blount, Alabama, United States (buried in Wynnville Cemetery). She married GEORGE FRANK MUSE. He was born in Sep 1879 in Carroll, County, Ga.. He died on 14 Sep 1957 in Blount, Alabama, USA.

11.   **ROBERT BENNETT**[3] **MOORE I** (Robert Marian[2], Zachariah[1]) was born on 16 Oct 1850 in Walton, Georgia, USA. He died on 03 Sep 1901 in Blount, Alabama, USA (Burial in Mt. Moriah Cemetery).

He married **SARAH ELIZABETH HICKS** on 21 Nov 1872 in Blount, Alabama. She was born on 21 Oct 1853 in Alabama, United States. She died on 13 Jun 1931 in Blount, Alabama, United States (Burial in Mt. Moriah Cem).

Robert Bennett Moore I and Sarah Elizabeth Hicks had the following children:

19.   i.   WILLIAM (GUS) AUGUSTUS[4] MOORE (son of Robert Bennett Moore I and Sarah Elizabeth Hicks) was born on 29 Apr 1875 in Blount, Alabama, USA. He died on 14 Apr 1956 in Blount Co.Alabama, USA (Burial in Mt. Moriah Cemetery). He married TERA H. COATS on 03 Nov 1897. She was born on 21 Sep 1875 in Alabama, United States. She died on 05 Feb 1932 in Susan Moore, Blount Co, Ala (Burial in Mt. Moriah Cemetery).

20.   ii.   VILLULA ARMELIA MOORE (daughter of Robert Bennett Moore I and Sarah Elizabeth Hicks) was born on 18 Jun 1878 in Blount, Alabama, USA. She died on 29 Jun 1924 in Blount Co.Alabama, USA. She married ARTHUR MARVIN PHILLIPS. He was born on 11 Jan 1880 in Blount, Alabama, United States. He died in Dec 1962 in Pennsylvania, United States.

        iii. VADA MAY MOORE (daughter of Robert Bennett Moore I and Sarah Elizabeth Hicks) was born on 02 Mar 1883 in Alabama. She died on 04 Dec 1907.

12.   **DAVID SANDERS**[3] **MOORE MD** (Robert Marian[2], Zachariah[1]) was born on 19 Mar 1852 in Near Lawrenceville, Walton County, GA. He died on 09 Dec 1932 in Blount, Alabama, USA (Wynnville Cem. Blount Co., AL). He married **SUSAN ALEXANDRIA NUNNALLEY** on 25 Mar 1875 in Blount, Alabama. She was born on 25 Sep 1854 in Georgia. She died on 01 Mar 1923 in Blount, Alabama, United States (Burial in Wynnville Cem.).

David Sanders Moore MD and Susan Alexandria Nunnalley had the following children:

         i.   TALIAFERRO CLARENCE[4] MOORE (son of David Sanders Moore MD and Susan Alexandria Nunnalley) was born on 29 Apr 1876 in Clarence, Blount County, Alabama. He died on 08 Jan 1923 in Jefferson, Alabama. He married CLINTON MONTGOMERY. She was born on 22 Sep 1879 in Blount Co.Alabama, USA. She died in May 1964 in Polk County, Florida, USA.

22.   ii.   ROBERT JACKSON 'BOB' MOORE (son of David Sanders Moore MD and Susan Alexandria Nunnalley) was born on 27 Oct 1877 in Alabama. He died on 26 Oct 1949 in Austin, Travis, Texas, USA (City Cemetery, Travis Texas, USA). He married ELEANOR H. WATSON about 1906. She was born on 02 Sep 1887 in Georgia. She died on 16 Aug 1946 in Bastrop, Texas.

23.   iii. MARY PEARL MOORE (daughter of David Sanders Moore MD and Susan Alexandria Nunnalley) was born on 12 Sep 1879 in Alabama. She died on 16 Jan 1934 in Jefferson, Alabama, USA. She married EUGENE OLIVER DEAN on 03 Jan 1901 in Blount, Alabama, United States. He was born on 27 Apr 1871 in Blount, Alabama, United States. He died on 04 Nov 1942 in Orange, Orange, Texas, USA.

        iv.   FLAVUS M. MOORE (son of David Sanders Moore MD and Susan Alexandria Nunnalley) was born on 27 Oct 1881 in Alabama. He died on 14 Jan 1897 in Susan Moore, Alabama, USA (Wynnville Cem. Blount Co., AL).

         v.   SUSAN FLORENCE MOORE (daughter of David Sanders Moore MD and Susan Alexandria Nunnalley) was born on 03 Mar 1883 in Alabama. She died on 05 Jan 1884 in Susan Moore, Alabama (Wynnville Cem. Blount Co., AL).

    vi.   DAVID S. MOORE JR. MD (son of David Sanders Moore MD and Susan Alexandria Nunnalley) was born on 11 Apr 1886 in Blount, Alabama, USA. He died on 09 Jun 1947 in Jefferson, Alabama.

    vii.   JOSEPH GROVER MOORE MD (son of David Sanders Moore MD and Susan Alexandria Nunnalley) was born on 10 Mar 1888 in Alabama. He died on 20 Jul 1953 in Birmingham, Alabama, USA (Burial in Elmwood Cemetery, Birmingham, AL USA). He married (1) CORNELIA MARTIN. He married (2) ESSIE MNU. He married (3) LUCILLE FORD.

    viii.   ALDON O. MOORE (son of David Sanders Moore MD and Susan Alexandria Nunnalley) was born on 18 Mar 1890 in Alabama. He died on 24 Sep 1908 in Susan Moore, Alabama, USA (Wynnville Cem. Blount Co., AL).

    ix.   EARL MOORE (son of David Sanders Moore MD and Susan Alexandria Nunnalley) was born on 19 Aug 1897 in Alabama. He died on 29 Aug 1899 in Susan Moore, Alabama (Wynnville Cem. Blount Co., AL).

13.   **BENJAMIN MARTIN**[3] **MOORE** (Robert Marian[2], Zachariah[1]) was born on 23 Mar 1854 in Walton Co. GA USA. He died on 25 Feb 1943 in Blount Co.Alabama, USA (Burial in Mt. Moriah Cemetery). He married **HAVANNA FANNIE SCRUGGS**. She was born on 07 Mar 1860 in Alabama, United States. She died on 19 Jan 1926 in Clarence, Blount, Alabama.

Benjamin Martin Moore and Havanna Fannie Scruggs had the following children:

23.   i. JAMES ROBERT[4] MOORE (son of Benjamin Martin Moore and Havanna Fannie Scruggs) was born on 07 Aug 1881 in Alabama. He died on 09 Jan 1963 in Oneonta, Blount, Alabama, USA. He married ANNIE SYLVAINIA BENTLEY.

24.   ii. MARY ETHEL MOORE (daughter of Benjamin Martin Moore and Havanna Fannie Scruggs) was born on 01 May 1883 in Alabama. She died on 19 Feb 1963 in Oneonta, Blount, Alabama. She married JESSE BURNS.

25.   iii. OLA FRANCES MOORE (daughter of Benjamin Martin Moore and Havanna Fannie Scruggs) was born on 01 Jul 1891 in Blount, Alabama, United States. She died on 09 Aug 1978 in Oneonta, Blount, Alabama, United States of America. She married ELDRIDGE DAILEY.

26.   iv. BEULAH ENNIS MOORE (daughter of Benjamin Martin Moore and Havanna Fannie Scruggs) was born on 15 Oct 1895 in Clarence, Blount Co., Alabama. She died on 08 Dec 1968 in Blount, Alabama, United States. She married JASPER ASBURY BYNUM. He was born on 25 Nov 1889. He died on 26 Mar 1961.

     v. BENNETT PLEMON MOORE (son of Benjamin Martin Moore and Havanna Fannie Scruggs) was born on 09 Jul 1896.

     vi. VERNIE LOIA MOORE (daughter of Benjamin Martin Moore and Havanna Fannie Scruggs) was born on 19 Oct 1897.

14.   **JOHN MORGAN**[3] **MOORE** (Robert Marian[2], Zachariah[1]) was born on 17 Sep 1855 in Monroe, Walton, Georgia. He died on 01 Aug 1935 in Blount, Alabama, USA (Burial in Mt. Moriah Cem). He married (1) **FANNIE COX**, daughter of Albert Ewing Cox and Juliet Warren Alford. She was born in 1859 in Georgia, United States. He married (2) **EMMA ENTREKIN** in Blount, Alabama. She was born in May 1870 in Georgia, United States. He married (3) **SUSAN MILLIE GRIFFIN**. She was born in Aug 1876 in , , Alabama, USA.

John Morgan Moore and Fannie Cox had the following children:

27.   i. JOEL WILLIAM[4] MOORE (son of John Morgan Moore and Fannie Cox) was born on 02 Sep 1879 in Alabama, United States. He died on 03 Jul 1930 in Travis, Texas, United States. He married (1) ROXIE PATE. She was born in 1885. She died in 1904 in Texas, United States. He married (2) CLEM DUNGAR. She was born on 17 Dec 1881 in Texas. She died on 01 Apr 1927.

        ii. MARION MOORE (son of John Morgan Moore and Fannie Cox) was born on 26 Nov 1882 in Alabama, United States. He died in May 1908.

15.   **DR. JAMES "JIMMY" HAMILTON**[3] **MOORE D.MD** (Robert Marian[2], Zachariah[1]) was born on 08 Mar 1858 in Walton, Georgia, USA. He died on 27 Mar 1939 in Blount, Alabama, USA (Burial in Mt. Moriah Cem). He married (1) **LEILA ISADORE MCDONALD** on 17 Feb 1881 in Blount County, Alabama, USA (Burial in Mt. Moriah Cemetery). She was born on 03 Dec 1864 in Alabama. She died on 18 Mar 1886 in Blount, AL, USA (Burial in Mt. Moriah Cemetery). He married (2) **ELEANOR E RAY** in 1888 in Blount, Alabama, United States (Burial in Mt. Moriah Cemetery), daughter of Moses (Maso) Ray and Elizabeth McDonald. She was born on 04 Nov 1869 in Alabama, United States. She died on 22 May 1890 in Blount, Alabama, United States (Burial in Mt. Moriah Cemetery). He married (3) **SAVANNAH VILULA BYNUM** in 1890 in Blount, Alabama, United States (Burial in Mt. Moriah Cemetery). She was born on 03 Dec 1870 in Blount, Alabama, United States.

She died on 16 Apr 1939 in Blount, Alabama, United States (Burial in Mt. Moriah Cemetery).

Dr. James "Jimmy" Hamilton Moore D.MD and Leila Isadore McDonald had the following children:

28.   i. CHARLES CLAUDE[4] MOORE (son of Dr. James "Jimmy" Hamilton Moore D.MD and Leila Isadore McDonald) was born on 15 Jan 1882 in Blount County, Alabama, USA. He died on 05 Jul 1962 in Blount Co.Alabama (Burial in Wynnville Cem.). He married ADA ETHEL LAMB on 09 Oct 1910 in Blount Co.Alabama, USA, daughter of James Sanford Lamb and Margaret Rebecca Scruggs. She was born on 31 Oct 1883 in Blount County, Alabama, USA. She died on 22 Jul 1950 in Oneonta, Blount, Alabama, USA (Burial in Wynnville Cem.).

        ii. ALICE M MOORE (daughter of Dr. James "Jimmy" Hamilton Moore D.MD and Leila Isadore McDonald) was born on 13 Apr 1884 in Blount County, AL. She died on 13 Jan 1885 in Blount County, Alabama, USA Buried at Mt Moriah Cemetery (First person buried in Mt. Moriah Cemetery).

        iii. INFANT MOORE (daughter of Dr. James "Jimmy" Hamilton Moore D.MD and Leila Isadore McDonald) was born in 1885. She died in 1885 in Susan Moore, Alabama, USA (Burial in Mt. Moriah Cemetery).

Dr. James "Jimmy" Hamilton Moore D.MD and Eleanor E Ray had the following child:

29.   iv. LULA LADORA DORA MOORE (daughter of Dr. James "Jimmy" Hamilton Moore D.MD and Eleanor E Ray) was born on 14 May 1890 in Alabama. She married WARREN DICKSON HOLLAND about 1911 in Blount, Alabama, USA. He was born on 19 Dec 1881 in Blount, Alabama, USA. He died in Oct 1973 in Guntersville, Marshall, Alabama, USA.

Dr. James "Jimmy" Hamilton Moore D.MD and Savannah Vilula Bynum had the following children:

        v. GENORA MOORE (daughter of Dr. James "Jimmy" Hamilton Moore D.MD and Savannah Vilula Bynum) was born on 13 Feb 1892 in Blount, Alabama, United States. She died on 06 Jun 1894 in Blount, Alabama, United States.

30.   vi. Susie Iola Moore (daughter of Dr. James "Jimmy" Hamilton Moore D.MD and Savannah Vilula Bynum) was born on 18 Oct 1894 in Alabama, United States. She died on 02 Aug 1966 in College Park, Fulton, Georgia, United States. She married Ersie Leon Eller in 1911. He was born on 18 Sep 1894 in Blount, Alabama, United States. He died on 31 Jul 1973 in Merriwether County, Georgia, United States.

31.   vii. James Carl Moore (son of Dr. James "Jimmy" Hamilton Moore D.MD and Savannah Vilula Bynum) was born on 10 Oct 1896 in Blount, Alabama, United States. He died on 06 Dec 1959 in Susan Moore, Alabama, United States (Burial in Mt. Moriah Cemetery). He married Pernie Light. She was born on 14 Sep 1898. She died on 14 Jul 1993 in Susan Moore, Alabama, United States (Burial in Mt. Moriah Cem).

        viii. William Cleo Moore (son of Dr. James "Jimmy" Hamilton Moore D.MD and Savannah Vilula Bynum) was born on 23 Aug 1898 in Alabama, United States. He died on 28 Sep 1957 in Wynnville Cem, Alabama, United States. He married Mae Bailey.

        ix. John David Jd Moore (son of Dr. James "Jimmy" Hamilton Moore D.MD and Savannah Vilula Bynum) was born on 23 Nov 1900 in Alabama, United States. He died on 22 Apr 1971.

        x. V Pearl Moore (daughter of Dr. James "Jimmy" Hamilton Moore D.MD and Savannah Vilula Bynum) was born on 06 Aug 1903. She died on 06 Aug 1906 in Mt Moriah Cem, Blount, Alabama, United States.

32.   xi. Robert Cayce Moore (son of Dr. James "Jimmy" Hamilton Moore D.MD and Savannah Vilula Bynum) was born on 09 Dec 1905 in Alabama, United States. He died on 29 Jul 1984 in Susan Moore, Alabama, United States (Burial in Mt. Moriah Cemetery). He married Le Merle Oliver. She was born about 1908. She died on 16 Jun 2001.

        xii. J Sanders Moore (son of Dr. James "Jimmy" Hamilton Moore D.MD and Savannah Vilula Bynum) was born on 06 May 1908 in Alabama, United States. He died on 07 Dec 1913 in Blount, Alabama, United States (Burial in Mt. Moriah Cemetery).

        xiii. Coy O Moore (son of Dr. James "Jimmy" Hamilton Moore D.MD and Savannah Vilula Bynum) was born on 18 Dec 1911. He died on 11 Oct 1914 in Blount, Alabama, United States (Burial in Mt. Moriah Cemetery).

16.   Daniel Marion[3] Moore (Robert Marian[2], Zachariah[1]) was born on 13 Aug 1859 in Walton, Georgia, USA. He died on 08 Sep 1942 in Blount, Alabama, USA. He married Marie Olga Malzie Green on 25 Feb 1883 in Blount, Alabama, USA. She was born on 18 Jun 1867 in Alabama, USA. She died on 22 Jun 1943 in Mon... Pt., Shelby, Alabama.

Daniel Marion Moore and Marie Olga Malzie Green had the following children:

33.   i.   ADDA VESTA^4 MOORE (daughter of Daniel Marion Moore and Marie Olga Malzie Green) was born on 14 Feb 1884 in Alabama. She died on 05 Jan 1972 in Birmingham, Jefferson, Alabama. She married SAMUEL ALEXANDER MURRAY. He was born on 14 Feb 1884 in Blount County, Alabama, USA. He died on 26 Feb 1969 in Birmingham, Jefferson, Alabama, United States of America.

34.   ii. WILLIAM OSCAR MOORE (son of Daniel Marion Moore and Marie Olga Malzie Green) was born on 10 Jul 1887 in Alabama, USA. He died on 26 Jun 1967 in Cleveland, Blount, Alabama, USA. He married DOCIA F BLACKWOOD. She was born about 1897 in Alabama. She died on 23 Apr 1962 in Cleveland, Blount, Alabama, United States.

35.   iii. VERNICE C. MOORE (daughter of Daniel Marion Moore and Marie Olga Malzie Green) was born on 17 Jul 1900 in Alabama. She died on 12 Jan 1996 in Arab, Marshall, Alabama, USA. She married LEWIS HERBON WHITE. He was born on 09 Nov 1896 in Alabama. He died on 02 Aug 1949 in Blount, Alabama, USA.

36.   iv. ROBERT BENNETT MOORE II (son of Daniel Marion Moore and Marie Olga Malzie Green) was born on 18 Jan 1903 in Alabama, USA. He died on 07 Nov 1957 in Oneonta, Blount, Alabama (Burial in Mt. Moriah Cemetery). He married CORNELIA B SLOMAN. She was born about 1905 in Georgia.

17. **NANCY A ELIZABETH^3 MOORE** (Robert Marian^2, Zachariah^1) was born on 13 Aug 1861 in Walton, Georgia, USA. She died on 22 Jun 1891 in Blount, Alabama, USA. She married **JOHN QUINCY ADAMS** on 17 Jul 1881 in Blount, Alabama, United States, son of Elijah Adams and Orenna Brown. He was born on 11 Nov 1858 in Dale, Alabama, United States. He died on 07 Sep 1919 in Blount, Alabama, United States.

John Quincy Adams and Nancy A Elizabeth Moore had the following children:

37.   i.   DONA PEARL DONIE^4 ADAMS (daughter of John Quincy Adams and Nancy A Elizabeth Moore) was born on 25 Jun 1882 in Blount, Alabama, United States. She died on 04 Jul 1971 in Blount, Alabama, USA. She married CHARLES HEZIKIAH HARVEY on 21 Mar 1909 in Clarence, Blount, Alabama, USA. He was born on 16 Aug 1882 in Blount, Alabama, USA. He died on 05 Feb 1919 in Blount, Alabama, USA.

        ii. NANCY LEE ADAMS (daughter of John Quincy Adams and Nancy A Elizabeth Moore) was born on 05 Sep 1883. She died on 09 May 1887.

38.   iii. NAPOLEON EUGENE ADAMS (son of John Quincy Adams and Nancy A Elizabeth Moore) was born on 28 Aug 1885 in Blount, Alabama, United States. He died on 28 Jan 1975 in Pasadena, Harris, Texas, United States. He married LETTIE BELLE TIDWELL, daughter of Evins G Tidwell and Mary Jane Young. She was born on 18 Feb 1888 in Blount, Alabama, USA. She died on 11 Feb 1976 in Pasadena, Harris, Texas, USA.

39.   iv. LABORN ELIJAH ADAMS (son of John Quincy Adams and Nancy A Elizabeth Moore) was born on 19 Jun 1886 in Clarence, Blount, Alabama, United States. He died on 02 Jul 1960. He married MAGGIE V LEWIS. She was born about 1886 in Alabama.

40.   v.   SALLY EMMER ABAGEL ADAMS (daughter of John Quincy Adams and Nancy A Elizabeth Moore) was born on 13 Apr 1889 in Clarence, Blount, Alabama, United States. She died on 31 Jul 1948 in Blount, Alabama, USA. She married DAVID STEVE B ARNES. He was born on 25 Mar 1886 in Brooksville, Blount, Alabama, USA. He died on 24 Feb 1970 in Oneonta, Blount, Alabama, United States of America.

      vi.   MILLEY J ADAMS (daughter of John Quincy Adams and Nancy A Elizabeth Moore) was born in Aug 1891 in Alabama.

     vii.   ELBERT H ADAMS (son of John Quincy Adams and Nancy A Elizabeth Moore) was born in Sep 1892 in Alabama.

    viii.   DOLLIE E ADAMS (daughter of John Quincy Adams and Nancy A Elizabeth Moore) was born in Feb 1895 in Alabama.

18.   **EMMA JANE MARY**[3] **MOORE** (Robert Marian[2], Zachariah[1]) was born on 08 Aug 1864 in Georgia, United States. She died on 12 Nov 1912 in Blount, Alabama, USA. She married **ASBERRY NEWTON BUD BALLARD**. He was born on 19 Mar 1861 in Mississippi, United States. He died on 05 Jun 1948.

Asberry Newton Bud Ballard and Emma Jane Mary Moore had the following children:

      i.   EARNEST A.[4] BALLARD (son of Asberry Newton Bud Ballard and Emma Jane Mary Moore) was born on 01 Jun 1883. He died on 05 Sep 1886 in Blount Co., Alabama. (Burial at Ebenezer Cmetery).

     ii.   VIOLA E JONES (daughter of Asberry Newton Bud Ballard and Emma Jane Mary Moore) was born in 1905 in Alabama, United States Adopted.

Generation 4

19.   **WILLIAM (GUS) AUGUSTUS**[4] **MOORE** (Robert Bennett[3] I, Robert Marian[2], Zachariah[1]) was born on 29 Apr 1875 in Blount, Alabama, USA. He died on 14 Apr 1956 in Blount Co.Alabama, USA (Burial in Mt. Moriah Cemetery). He married **TERA H. COATS** on 03 Nov 1897. She was born on 21 Sep 1875 in Alabama, United States. She died on 05 Feb 1932 in Susan Moore, Blount Co, Ala (Burial in Mt. Moriah Cemetery).

William (Gus) Augustus Moore and Tera H. Coats had the following children:

      i.   MOORE (daughter of William (Gus) Augustus Moore and Tera H. Coats) was born on 12 Jan 1889. She died on 12 Jan 1889.

41.   ii. ETOILE E MOORE (daughter of William (Gus) Augustus Moore and Tera H. Coats) was born on 23 Oct 1901 in Blount Co.Alabama, USA. She died on 05 Mar 1993 in Susan Moore, Blount, Alabama, USA (Burial in Mt. Moriah Cemetery). She married ORRIS H. MARTIN. He was born on 17 Jun 1904. He died on 30 Nov 1970 in Susan Moore, Blount Co, Ala (Burial in Mt. Moriah Cemetery).

20.   **VILLULA ARMELIA**[4] **MOORE** (Robert Bennett[3] I, Robert Marian[2], Zachariah[1]) was born on 18 Jun 1878 in Blount, Alabama, USA. She died on 29 Jun 1924 in Blount Co.Alabama, USA. She married **ARTHUR MARVIN PHILLIPS**. He was born on 11 Jan 1880 in Blount, Alabama, United States. He died in Dec 1962 in Pennsylvania, United States.

Arthur Marvin PHILLIPS and Villula Armelia Moore had the following children:

42.   i. AUBREY[5] PHILLIPS (son of Arthur Marvin PHILLIPS and Villula Armelia Moore) was born about 1915. He died on 06 Mar 1966 in Birmingham, Jefferson, Alabama. He married CECILIA JOHNSTON.

43.   ii. OPAL PHILLIPS (daughter of Arthur Marvin PHILLIPS and Villula Armelia Moore) was born on 02 May 1916. She married BILL LANIER.

44.   iii. ARTHUR PHILLIPS JR. (son of Arthur Marvin PHILLIPS and Villula Armelia Moore). He married LENA HUDSON.

45. iv. COY B PHILLIPS (son of Arthur Marvin PHILLIPS and Villula Armelia Moore) was born in 1905 in Alabama, United States. He married ADALINE MNU.

46. v. ROY C PHILLIPS (son of Arthur Marvin PHILLIPS and Villula Armelia Moore) was born in 1906 in Alabama, United States. He married MNU.

vi. RUBYE M PHILLIPS (daughter of Arthur Marvin PHILLIPS and Villula Armelia Moore) was born on 21 May 1908 in Alabama, United States. She married RAYMOND BAYLISS.

47. vii. SARA PEARL PHILLIPS (daughter of Arthur Marvin PHILLIPS and Villula Armelia Moore) was born on 04 Jul 1910 in Altoona, Etowah, Alabama, United States. She died on 22 Sep 1961 in Foley, Baldwin, Alabama, United States. She married WILLIAM JORDAN GULLEDGE on 22 Sep 1927 in Baldwin, Alabama, United States. He was born on 03 Jan 1905 in Rosinton, Alabama, United States. He died on 02 May 1990 in Robertsdale, Baldwin, Alabama, United States.

48. viii. GRADY WOODROW PHILLIPS (son of Arthur Marvin PHILLIPS and Villula Armelia Moore) was born on 16 May 1919 in Alabama, United States. He died on 20 Jul 2008 in Dallas, Dallas, Texas, United States. He married DORRIS COCKERHAM.

21. ROBERT JACKSON 'BOB'[4] MOORE (David Sanders[3] MD, Robert Marian[2], Zachariah[1]) was born on 27 Oct 1877 in Alabama. He died on 26 Oct 1949 in Austin, Travis, Texas, USA (City Cemetery, Travis Texas, USA). He married ELEANOR H. WATSON about 1906. She was born on 02 Sep 1887 in Georgia. She died on 16 Aug 1946 in Bastrop, Texas.

Robert Jackson 'Bob' Moore and Eleanor H. Watson had the following child:

i. ELEANOR MERLE 'MERLE'[5] MOORE (daughter of Robert Jackson 'Bob' Moore and Eleanor H. Watson) was born about 1909 in Texas. She married SMITH.

22. MARY PEARL[4] MOORE (David Sanders[3] MD, Robert Marian[2], Zachariah[1]) was born on 12 Sep 1879 in Alabama. She died on 16 Jan 1934 in Jefferson, Alabama, USA. She married EUGENE OLIVER DEAN on 03 Jan 1901 in Blount, Alabama, United States. He was born on 27 Apr 1871 in Blount, Alabama, United States. He died on 04 Nov 1942 in Orange, Orange, Texas, USA.

Eugene Oliver Dean and Mary Pearl Moore had the following children:

i. FANNY MOORE[5] DEAN (daughter of Eugene Oliver Dean and Mary Pearl Moore) was born in 1902 in Texas, United States.

ii. JOHN DAVID DEAN (son of Eugene Oliver Dean and Mary Pearl Moore) was born on 10 Oct 1903 in Texas, United States. He died on 25 Mar 1939 in Early, Georgia, United States.

iii. LUCILLE DEAN (daughter of Eugene Oliver Dean and Mary Pearl Moore) was born in 1906 in Texas, United States.

iv. ELLIS DEAN (son of Eugene Oliver Dean and Mary Pearl Moore) was born about 1909 in New Mexico. He died on 25 May 1956.

23. JAMES ROBERT[4] MOORE (Benjamin Martin[3], Robert Marian[2], Zachariah[1]) was born on 07 Aug 1881 in Alabama. He died on 09 Jan 1963 in Oneonta, Blount, Alabama, USA. He married ANNIE SYLVAINIA BENTLEY.

James Robert Moore and Annie Sylvainia Bentley had the following child:

49. i. EDWIN LEON[5] MOORE (son of James Robert Moore and Annie Sylvainia Bentley) was born on 05 May 1906 in Union Point,AL. He married (1) GUSSIE RASCO on 17 Jul 1928. He married (3) GUSSIE RASCO.

24. **MARY ETHEL**[4] **MOORE** (Benjamin Martin[3], Robert Marian[2], Zachariah[1]) was born on 01 May 1883 in Alabama. She died on 19 Feb 1963 in Oneonta, Blount, Alabama. She married **JESSE BURNS**.

Jesse Burns and Mary Ethel Moore had the following children:

50. i. CLARA[5] BURNS (daughter of Jesse Burns and Mary Ethel Moore). She married JOE B. GUNNELLS.
51. ii. JEROME J. BURNS (son of Jesse Burns and Mary Ethel Moore). He married EVELYN WHITE.
     iii. MARTHA FRANCES BURNS (daughter of Jesse Burns and Mary Ethel Moore).
52. iv. MERLE BURNS (daughter of Jesse Burns and Mary Ethel Moore). She married WALTER MAJORS.
     v. TWINS BURNS (child of Jesse Burns and Mary Ethel Moore).

25. **OLA FRANCES**[4] **MOORE** (Benjamin Martin[3], Robert Marian[2], Zachariah[1]) was born on 01 Jul 1891 in Blount, Alabama, United States. She died on 09 Aug 1978 in Oneonta, Blount, Alabama, United States of America. She married **ELDRIDGE DAILEY**.

Eldridge Dailey and Ola Frances Moore had the following children:

     i. VERRELL[5] DAILEY (daughter of Eldridge Dailey and Ola Frances Moore).
     ii. DRERELL DAILEY (son of Eldridge Dailey and Ola Frances Moore). He married DORIS WALLS.
     iii. DOROTHY DAILEY (daughter of Eldridge Dailey and Ola Frances Moore). She married CHARLES FORMBY.
53. iv. MAX DAILEY (son of Eldridge Dailey and Ola Frances Moore). He married JEAN INGRAM.

26. **BEULAH ENNIS**[4] **MOORE** (Benjamin Martin[3], Robert Marian[2], Zachariah[1]) was born on 15 Oct 1895 in Clarence, Blount Co., Alabama. She died on 08 Dec 1968 in Blount, Alabama, United States. She married **JASPER ASBURY BYNUM**. He was born on 25 Nov 1889. He died on 26 Mar 1961.

Jasper Asbury Bynum and Beulah Ennis Moore had the following children:

54. i. RALPH MOORE[5] BYNUM (son of Jasper Asbury Bynum and Beulah Ennis Moore). He married SYBLE COLE.
     ii. BOBBY PAUL BYNUM (son of Jasper Asbury Bynum and Beulah Ennis Moore). He married NORMA BROWN.
55. iii. RACHEL BYNUM (daughter of Jasper Asbury Bynum and Beulah Ennis Moore). She married LUTHER BENTLEY JR..
56. iv. FANNIE NAN BYNUM (daughter of Jasper Asbury Bynum and Beulah Ennis Moore). She married JOHNNY DAVIS.

27. **JOEL WILLIAM**[4] **MOORE** (John Morgan[3], Robert Marian[2], Zachariah[1]) was born on 02 Sep 1879 in Alabama, United States. He died on 03 Jul 1930 in Travis, Texas, United States. He married (1) **ROXIE PATE**. She was born in 1885. She died in 1904 in Texas, United States.

He married (2) **CLEM DUNGAR**. She was born on 17 Dec 1881 in Texas. She died on 01 Apr 1927.

Joel William Moore and Roxie Pate had the following child:

      i. ROXIE[5] MOORE (daughter of Joel William Moore and Roxie Pate) was born in 1905 in Alabama. She died in Died in Texas.

Joel William Moore and Clem Dungar had the following children:

      ii. JOEL HOWARD MOORE (son of Joel William Moore and Clem Dungar) was born on 15 May 1910. He died on 26 Oct 1910 in Bastrop, Texas.

      iii. JOHN LESTER MOORE (son of Joel William Moore and Clem Dungar) was born on 30 May 1913 in Mcdale, Texas, United States. He died on 30 Aug 1960 in Rockdale, Milam, Texas, United States.

28. **CHARLES CLAUDE**[4] **MOORE** (Dr. James "Jimmy" Hamilton[3] D.MD, Robert Marian[2], Zachariah[1]) was born on 15 Jan 1882 in Blount County, Alabama, USA. He died on 05 Jul 1962 in Blount Co.Alabama (Burial in Wynnville Cem.). He married **ADA ETHEL LAMB** on 09 Oct 1910 in Blount Co.Alabama, USA, daughter of James Sanford Lamb and Margaret Rebecca Scruggs. She was born on 31 Oct 1883 in Blount County, Alabama, USA. She died on 22 Jul 1950 in Oneonta, Blount, Alabama, USA (Burial in Wynnville Cem.).

Charles Claude Moore and Ada Ethel Lamb had the following children:

57. i. CONSTANCE IVALEEN[5] MOORE (daughter of Charles Claude Moore and Ada Ethel Lamb) was born on 13 Dec 1911 in Blount County, Alabama, USA. She died on 07 Nov 1993 in Oneonta, AL USA Buried in Marshall Memory Gardens, Marshall, Alabama, United States. She married ZOLEN TRACY CURREY on 26 Mar 1939 in Marshall County, Alabama, USA. He was born on 06 Oct 1905 in Marshall County,

Alabama, USA. He died on 06 Oct 1995 in Oneonta, Blount, Alabama, USA.

58. ii. LEILA REBECCA MOORE (daughter of Charles Claude Moore and Ada Ethel Lamb) was born on 13 Oct 1913 in Alabama. She died on 25 Mar 2001 in Antioch Church of Christ. She married CONNIE HARLEY MILLER on 17 Dec 1938. He was born on 22 Apr 1906.

59. iii. ADA ETHEL MOORE (daughter of Charles Claude Moore and Ada Ethel Lamb) was born on 28 Jun 1920 in Blount County. She married CHARLES RENFRO ODEN. He was born on 25 Apr 1919. He died on 01 Apr 2003.

29. **LULA LADORA DORA**[4] **MOORE** (Dr. James "Jimmy" Hamilton[3] D.MD, Robert Marian[2], Zachariah[1]) was born on 14 May 1890 in Alabama. She married **WARREN DICKSON HOLLAND** about 1911 in Blount, Alabama, USA. He was born on 19 Dec 1881 in Blount, Alabama, USA. He died in Oct 1973 in Guntersville, Marshall, Alabama, USA.

Warren Dickson Holland and Lula Ladora Dora Moore had the following children:

60. i. HENRY GRADY[5] HOLLAND (son of Warren Dickson Holland and Lula Ladora Dora Moore) was born on 20 Sep 1911 in Blount County, Alabama, USA. He died on 01 Aug 1992 in Gadsden, Etowah, Alabama, USA. He married CLEO FREEMAN. She was born on 28 Jan 1920 in Hamilton County, Tennessee, USA. She died on 23 Mar 2010 in Gadsden, Etowah, Alabama, USA.

61. ii. RAY KYTLE HOLLAND SR. (son of Warren Dickson Holland and Lula Ladora Dora Moore) was born on 26 Sep 1912 in Alabama. He died on 29 Dec 1963 in Gadsden, Etowah, Alabama. He married BART KELLY. She was born on 15 Jun 1911 in Marshall County, Alabama, USA. She died on 08 Dec 2003 in Gadsden, Etowah, Alabama, USA.

62.   iii. JAMES B HOLLAND (son of Warren Dickson Holland and Lula Ladora Dora Moore) was born about 1916 in Alabama. He married FLORENCE BENZ.

iv.   CLEONE M HOLLAND (daughter of Warren Dickson Holland and Lula Ladora Dora Moore) was born in 1917. She married (1) BILL MILLER. She married (2) LESTER AYERS.

63.   v. L SANDERS HOLLAND (son of Warren Dickson Holland and Lula Ladora Dora Moore) was born about 1921 in Alabama. He married GLADYS HARDER.

64.   vi. C AVONELL HOLLAND (daughter of Warren Dickson Holland and Lula Ladora Dora Moore) was born about 1924 in Alabama. She married (2) ROSS SMITH.

65.   vii. W EVERETT "PUG" HOLLAND (son of Warren Dickson Holland and Lula Ladora Dora Moore) was born about 1926 in Alabama. He married LOIS ALLISON.

viii.   MARY E HOLLAND (daughter of Warren Dickson Holland and Lula Ladora Dora Moore) was born about 1929 in Alabama. She married JACK KEARNEY.

30.   SUSIE IOLA[4] MOORE (Dr. James "Jimmy" Hamilton[3] D.MD, Robert Marian[2], Zachariah[1]) was born on 18 Oct 1894 in Alabama, United States. She died on 02 Aug 1966 in College Park, Fulton, Georgia, United States. She married ERSIE LEON ELLER in 1911. He was born on 18 Sep 1894 in Blount, Alabama, United States. He died on 31 Jul 1973 in Merriwether County, Georgia, United States.

Ersie Leon Eller and Susie Iola Moore had the following children:

66.   i. VALERIA[5] ELLER (daughter of Ersie Leon Eller and Susie Iola Moore) was born about 1916 in Alabama. She died on 13 Jul 1995 in Clayton, Georgia. She married EUGENE OGLE.

67.   ii. OSMOND ELLER (son of Ersie Leon Eller and Susie Iola Moore) was born about 1919 in Alabama. He married ALLENE ADAMSON.

68.   iii. LILLIAN ELLER (daughter of Ersie Leon Eller and Susie Iola Moore) was born about 1923 in Alabama. She married GEORGE PRICHARD.

69.   iv. GRACE ELLER (daughter of Ersie Leon Eller and Susie Iola Moore) was born in 1928 in Georgia. She married ARTHUR BENEFIELD, son of Oscar Benefield and Lillie Sorrells. He was born on 29 Sep 1925 in Decatur, Georgia. He died on 03 Nov 1994 in East Point, Fulton County, Georgia.

31.   JAMES CARL[4] MOORE (Dr. James "Jimmy" Hamilton[3] D.MD, Robert Marian[2], Zachariah[1]) was born on 10 Oct 1896 in Blount, Alabama, United States. He died on 06 Dec 1959 in Susan Moore, Alabama, United States (Burial in Mt. Moriah Cemetery). He married PERNIE LIGHT. She was born on 14 Sep 1898. She died on 14 Jul 1993 in Susan Moore, Alabama, United States (Burial in Mt. Moriah Cem).

James Carl Moore and Pernie Light had the following children:

70.   i. JAMES CARL "JIMMY"[5] MOORE (son of James Carl Moore and Pernie Light) was born about 1929 in Alabama. He married JANE BROCK.

ii.   TALMAGE H MOORE (son of James Carl Moore and Pernie Light) was born on 12 Apr 1931. He died on 08 Mar 2008 in Guntersville, Marshall, Alabama, United States. He married CAROLYN HULLETT.

32. **ROBERT CAYCE**[4] **MOORE** (Dr. James "Jimmy" Hamilton[3] D.MD, Robert Marian[2], Zachariah[1]) was born on 09 Dec 1905 in Alabama, United States. He died on 29 Jul 1984 in Susan Moore, Alabama, United States (Burial in Mt. Moriah Cemetery). He married **LE MERLE OLIVER**. She was born about 1908. She died on 16 Jun 2001.

Robert Cayce Moore and Le Merle Oliver had the following child:

71.   i.   ROBERT C. (BOB)[5] MOORE JR. (son of Robert Cayce Moore and Le Merle Oliver) was born on 12 Jul 1946. He married BETTY POSEY. She was born on 20 Dec 1946.

33. **ADDA VESTA**[4] **MOORE** (Daniel Marion[3], Robert Marian[2], Zachariah[1]) was born on 14 Feb 1884 in Alabama. She died on 05 Jan 1972 in Birmingham, Jefferson, Alabama. She married **SAMUEL ALEXANDER MURRAY**. He was born on 14 Feb 1884 in Blount County, Alabama, USA. He died on 26 Feb 1969 in Birmingham, Jefferson, Alabama, United States of America.

Samuel Alexander Murray and Adda Vesta Moore had the following children:

72.   i.   EARL OLIVER[5] MURRAY (son of Samuel Alexander Murray and Adda Vesta Moore) was born on 02 Sep 1902 in Alabama. He died on 05 Feb 1972 in Birmingham, Jefferson, Alabama, United States of America. He married ARTIE MAE LONG on 06 Sep 1926 in Cherokee Co, AL. She was born on 15 Jan 1909 in Georgia. She died on 24 Mar 1970 in Birmingham, Jefferson, Alabama, United States of America.

      ii.   RUTH M MURRAY (daughter of Samuel Alexander Murray and Adda Vesta Moore) was born on 15 Sep 1905 in Alabama, USA. She died on 07 Sep 1993 in Fort Myers, Lee, Florida, United States of America. She married ADOLPHUS JASPER RATLIFF. He was born on 26 Mar 1895 in Alabama, USA. He died on 22 Jan 1994 in Fort Myers, Lee, Florida, United States of America.

      iii. ERMAN MURRAY (son of Samuel Alexander Murray and Adda Vesta Moore) was born on 20 Jul 1908. He died on 24 Jan 1909.

73.   iv.   THOMAS HERMAN MURRAY (son of Samuel Alexander Murray and Adda Vesta Moore) was born on 20 Jul 1908 in Alabama, USA. He died on 16 Sep 1984 in North Augusta, Aiken, South Carolina, United States of America. He married MARY GLADYS CHAFFIN on 18 Mar 1928 in Lawrence, Tennessee. She was born on 19 Mar 1907 in Tennessee. She died on 14 Nov 1987 in Charleston, Charleston, South Carolina, United States of America.

      v.   RUBY MURRAY (daughter of Samuel Alexander Murray and Adda Vesta Moore) was born on 14 Jun 1911 in Alabama. She died on 25 Sep 1917 in Alabama, United States.

74.   vi.   CORNELIA IRENE MURRAY (daughter of Samuel Alexander Murray and Adda Vesta Moore) was born on 16 Jul 1919 in Alabama, USA. She died on 02 Jul 2011 in Germantown, Shelby, Tennessee, USA. She married ARTHUR JAMES MARSON.

34. **WILLIAM OSCAR**[4] **MOORE** (Daniel Marion[3], Robert Marian[2], Zachariah[1]) was born on 10 Jul 1887 in Alabama, USA. He died on 26 Jun 1967 in Cleveland, Blount, Alabama, USA. He married **DOCIA F BLACKWOOD**. She was born about 1897 in Alabama. She died on 23 Apr 1962 in Cleveland, Blount, Alabama, United States.

William Oscar Moore and Docia F Blackwood had the following children:

75.   i. IMOGENE F^5 MOORE (daughter of William Oscar Moore and Docia F Blackwood) was born on 12 Aug 1917 in Alabama. She died on 21 Dec 1996 in Deatsville, Elmore, Alabama, United States of America. She married JESSIE J WHITWORTH. He was born on 28 Jun 1917. He died in Jun 1983 in Blountsville, Blount, Alabama, United States of America.

76.   ii. V MAXINE MOORE (son of William Oscar Moore and Docia F Blackwood) was born about 1922 in Alabama. He died on 20 Dec 2003 in Birmingham, Jefferson, Alabama, USA. He married SYLVIA HIPP.

77.   iii. DORA J MOORE (daughter of William Oscar Moore and Docia F Blackwood) was born about 1926 in Alabama. She married JAMES C. HALLMARK.

35.   **VERNICE C.^{4} MOORE** (Daniel Marion^3, Robert Marian^2, Zachariah^1) was born on 17 Jul 1900 in Alabama. She died on 12 Jan 1996 in Arab, Marshall, Alabama, USA. She married **LEWIS HERBON WHITE**. He was born on 09 Nov 1896 in Alabama. He died on 02 Aug 1949 in Blount, Alabama, USA.

Lewis Herbon White and Vernice C. Moore had the following children:

78.   i. BARBARA ANN^5 WHITE (daughter of Lewis Herbon White and Vernice C. Moore). She married ADOLPHOUS FREDERICK WILSON.

     ii. CORNELIA MOORE WHITE (daughter of Lewis Herbon White and Vernice C. Moore) was born in 1921. She died in 1923.

79.   iii. LEWIS HERBON WHITE JR (son of Lewis Herbon White and Vernice C. Moore) was born on 28 Nov 1923 in Alabama. He died on 18 Dec 1973 in Blountsville, Alabama, USA. He married EVA YVONNE DOBSON. She was born on 28 Feb 1927. She died on 05 Mar 2010 in Oxford, Alabama, USA.

80.   iv. RUBY J WHITE (daughter of Lewis Herbon White and Vernice C. Moore) was born about 1928 in Alabama. She married JOE BAIN MARTIN.

     v. WILDA M WHITE (daughter of Lewis Herbon White and Vernice C. Moore) was born about 1930 in Alabama. She married BAMA M. CARR.

36.   **ROBERT BENNETT^4 MOORE II** (Daniel Marion^3, Robert Marian^2, Zachariah^1) was born on 18 Jan 1903 in Alabama, USA. He died on 07 Nov 1957 in Oneonta, Blount, Alabama (Burial in Mt. Moriah Cemetery). He married **CORNELIA B SLOMAN**. She was born about 1905 in Georgia.

Robert Bennett Moore II and Cornelia B Sloman had the following children:

81.   i. ARNELL E^5 MOORE (son of Robert Bennett Moore II and Cornelia B Sloman) was born about 1924 in Alabama. He married MILDRED NIBBLET.

82.   ii. WONDALINE MOORE (daughter of Robert Bennett Moore II and Cornelia B Sloman) was born about 1926 in Alabama. She married GERALD RIDGEWAY.

37.   **DONA PEARL DONIE^4 ADAMS** (Nancy A Elizabeth^3 Moore, Robert Marian^2 Moore, Zachariah^1 Moore) was born on 25 Jun 1882 in Blount, Alabama, United States. She died on 04 Jul 1971 in Blount, Alabama, USA. She married **CHARLES HEZIKIAH HARVEY** on 21 Mar 1909 in Clarence, Blount, Alabama, USA. He was born on 16 Aug 1882 in Blount, Alabama, USA. He died on 05 Feb 1919 in Blount, Alabama, USA.

Charles Hezikiah Harvey and Dona Pearl Donie Adams had the following children:

83.   i.   ATTICE LOLA[5] HARVEY (daughter of Charles Hezikiah Harvey and Dona Pearl Donie Adams) was born on 16 Apr 1910 in Blount, Alabama, USA. She died on 21 Jul 1969 in Altoona, Etowah, Alabama, USA. She married CONNIE MACK SHELTON. He was born on 22 Dec 1910 in Brooksville, Blount, Alabama, USA. He died on 08 Dec 1961 in Cullman, Cullman, Alabama.

84.   ii.   BRADY CORDELL HARVEY (son of Charles Hezikiah Harvey and Dona Pearl Donie Adams) was born on 02 May 1911 in Blount, Alabama, USA. He died on 15 Jan 2006 in Altoona, Etowah, Alabama, USA. He married BERNICE WAID on 23 Dec 1932. She was born on 23 Aug 1912 in Blountsville, Blount, AL, USA. She died on 02 Jun 1998 in Altoona, Etowah, AL.

      iii.   WILBURN TRESSIE HARVEY (son of Charles Hezikiah Harvey and Dona Pearl Donie Adams) was born on 12 Apr 1913 in Blount, Alabama, USA. He died on 09 Jun 1993 in Birmingham, Jefferson, Alabama, USA. He married HAZEL SIMMONS.

      iv.   BESSIE LEE HARVEY (daughter of Charles Hezikiah Harvey and Dona Pearl Donie Adams) was born on 18 Jun 1914. She died on 12 Feb 1919.

      v.   TOLLIVER HEZIKIAH HARVEY (son of Charles Hezikiah Harvey and Dona Pearl Donie Adams) was born on 29 Dec 1917. He died on 12 Feb 1919.

38.   **NAPOLEON EUGENE[4] ADAMS** (Nancy A Elizabeth[3] Moore, Robert Marian[2] Moore, Zachariah[1] Moore) was born on 28 Aug 1885 in Blount, Alabama, United States. He died on 28 Jan 1975 in Pasadena, Harris, Texas, United States. He married **LETTIE BELLE TIDWELL**, daughter of Evins G Tidwell and Mary Jane Young. She was born on 18 Feb 1888 in Blount, Alabama, USA. She died on 11 Feb 1976 in Pasadena, Harris, Texas, USA.

Napoleon Eugene Adams and Lettie Belle Tidwell had the following children:

      i.   REED[5] ADAMS (son of Napoleon Eugene Adams and Lettie Belle Tidwell) was born about 1909 in Alabama. He married KATE LOWERY.

86.   ii.   SPUD EARL ADAMS (son of Napoleon Eugene Adams and Lettie Belle Tidwell) was born about 1914 in Alabama. He married MAURINE TALTON.

      iii.   HUBERT ADAMS (son of Napoleon Eugene Adams and Lettie Belle Tidwell) was born about 1918 in Alabama. He married MINNIE TERRY.

      iv.   LUCY ADAMS (daughter of Napoleon Eugene Adams and Lettie Belle Tidwell) was born about 1919. She married CLAUDE GIBBONS.

86.   v.   LYDOTH ADAMS (daughter of Napoleon Eugene Adams and Lettie Belle Tidwell) was born about 1920 in Alabama. She married DOUGLASS STEFFANAUER.

39.   **LABORN ELIJAH[4] ADAMS** (Nancy A Elizabeth[3] Moore, Robert Marian[2] Moore, Zachariah[1] Moore) was born on 19 Jun 1886 in Clarence, Blount, Alabama, United States. He died on 02 Jul 1960. He married **MAGGIE V LEWIS**. She was born about 1886 in Alabama.

Laborn Elijah Adams and Maggie V Lewis had the following children:

87.   i.   GUSSIE LEWIS[5] ADAMS (son of Laborn Elijah Adams and Maggie V Lewis) was born on 05 Sep 1904 in Susan Moore, Blount, Alabama, United States. He died on 08 Nov 1995 in Arab, Marshall, Alabama, United States. He married ANNIE RUBY JONES. She was born on 14 Aug 1924 in Brooksville, Blount, Alabama, United States. She died on 19 Feb 2004 in Arab, Marshall, Alabama, United States.

88.   ii. ALDIE ADAMS (son of Laborn Elijah Adams and Maggie V Lewis) was born in 1908 in Alabama, United States. He died on 26 Jun 1981 in Ashtabula County, Ohio, USA. He married L ETHEL HILL. She was born about 1909 in Alabama.

89.   iii. ELLIS ADAMS (son of Laborn Elijah Adams and Maggie V Lewis) was born in 1910 in Alabama, United States. He died in Jun 1983 in Horton, Marshall, Alabama, United States of America. He married (1) ANDERSON. He married (2) EUNICE SLOMAN. She was born about 1903 in Alabama.

90.   iv. MACK ADAMS (son of Laborn Elijah Adams and Maggie V Lewis) was born on 15 Apr 1911 in Brooksville, Blount, Alabama, United States. He died on 15 Feb 1994 in Oneonta, Blount, Alabama, United States. He married ILA BEATRICE DOYLE on 20 Apr 1929 in Blount, Alabama, United States. She was born on 08 Aug 1909 in Brooksville, Blount, Alabama, United States. She died on 06 Nov 1991 in Birmingham, Jefferson, Alabama, United States.

    v. O CORENE ADAMS (daughter of Laborn Elijah Adams and Maggie V Lewis) was born in 1913 in Alabama. She married (1) VERBON FOUNTAIN. She married (2) GOLDEN DENDY.

91.   vi. LENA ADAMS (daughter of Laborn Elijah Adams and Maggie V Lewis) was born about 1915 in Alabama. She married DELBERT BESHEARS, son of WILLIE WILKS BESHEARS and LUCY j KERR. He was born in Aug 1914 in Blount County, Alabama, USA. He died on 14 Apr 1984 in Gadsden, Alabama, USA.

92.   vii. V JO ADAMS (daughter of Laborn Elijah Adams and Maggie V Lewis) was born about 1918 in Alabama. She married HENRY BROWN.

93.   viii. RECTOR ADAMS (son of Laborn Elijah Adams and Maggie V Lewis) was born in 1920 in Alabama. He died in 2008. He married EVE MARTIS.

94.   ix. C PEARL ADAMS (daughter of Laborn Elijah Adams and Maggie V Lewis) was born about 1924 in Alabama. She married TEAGUE.

40.   **SALLY EMMER ABAGEL**[4] **ADAMS** (Nancy A Elizabeth[3] Moore, Robert Marian[2] Moore, Zachariah[1] Moore) was born on 13 Apr 1889 in Clarence, Blount, Alabama, United States. She died on 31 Jul 1948 in Blount, Alabama, USA. She married **DAVID STEVE BARNES**. He was born on 25 Mar 1886 in Brooksville, Blount, Alabama, USA. He died on 24 Feb 1970 in Oneonta, Blount, Alabama, United States of America.

David Steve Barnes and Sally Emmer Abagel Adams had the following children:

95.   i. EULAS FLARE[5] BARNES (son of David Steve Barnes and Sally Emmer Abagel Adams) was born on 05 Feb 1909 in Clarence, Blount, Alabama, USA. He died on 18 Apr 1990 in Pinson, Alabama, USA. He married IRENE SIMMONS. She was born on 07 Sep 1910 in Pinson, Alabama, USA. She died on 19 Aug 1998 in Pinson, Alabama, USA.

96.   ii. PLUMIE BARNES (daughter of David Steve Barnes and Sally Emmer Abagel Adams) was born on 06 Sep 1910 in Blount County, Alabama, USA. She died on 02 Jul 2010 in Birmingham, Jefferson, Alabama, USA. She married GEORGE HUSTON BESHEARS in 1928. He was born on 20 Jul 1911 in Alabama. He died on 06 Jul 1992 in Gadsden, Alabama.

    iii. TUMIE CLASSAN BARNES (son of David Steve Barnes and Sally Emmer Abagel Adams) was born on 14 May 1914 in Clarence, Blount, Alabama, United States. He died on 23 Mar 1999 in Oneonta, Blount, Alabama, United States. He married ADA GERTRUDE WHITED. She was born on 08 Mar 1919 in Blount, Alabama, United States. She died on 14 Oct 1965 in Blount, Alabama, United States.

97.   iv.   OREN E BARNES (son of David Steve Barnes and Sally Emmer Abagel Adams) was born on 07 Jun 1922 in Clarence, Blount, Alabama, USA. He died on 22 Oct 1977 in Birmingham, Jefferson, Alabama, USA. He married ZIZ BLAIR.

98.   v.   MARY LOU BARNES (daughter of David Steve Barnes and Sally Emmer Abagel Adams) was born on 29 Aug 1928 in Clarence, Blount, Alabama, USA. She died on 12 May 2010 in Gadsden, Etowah, Alabama, United States of America. She married HERBERT BUICE.

      vi.   LOIS BARNES (daughter of David Steve Barnes and Sally Emmer Abagel Adams). She died before 1973.

      vii.   ALLEN BARNES (son of David Steve Barnes and Sally Emmer Abagel Adams). He died before 1973.

Generation 5

41.   ETOILE E^5 MOORE (William (Gus) Augustus^4, Robert Bennett^3 I, Robert Marian^2, Zachariah^1) was born on 23 Oct 1901 in Blount Co.Alabama, USA. She died on 05 Mar 1993 in Susan Moore, Blount, Alabama, USA (Burial in Mt. Moriah Cemetery). She married ORRIS H. MARTIN. He was born on 17 Jun 1904. He died on 30 Nov 1970 in Susan Moore, Blount Co, Ala (Burial in Mt. Moriah Cemetery).

Orris H. Martin and Etoile E Moore had the following child:

99.   i.   WILLIAM "BILLY" MOORE^6 MARTIN (son of Orris H. Martin and Etoile E Moore). He married (1) LUCILLE WHITED. He married (2) GERTHA BEASELY.

42.   AUBREY^5 PHILLIPS (Villula Armelia^4 Moore, Robert Bennett^3 Moore I, Robert Marian^2 Moore, Zachariah^1 Moore) was born about 1915. He died on 06 Mar 1966 in Birmingham, Jefferson, Alabama. He married CECILIA JOHNSTON.

Aubrey PHILLIPS and Cecilia Johnston had the following children:

      i.   PEARL^6 PHILLIPS (daughter of Aubrey PHILLIPS and Cecilia Johnston).

      ii.   KENNY PHILLIPS (son of Aubrey PHILLIPS and Cecilia Johnston).

      iii.   DANNY PHILLIPS (son of Aubrey PHILLIPS and Cecilia Johnston).

43.   OPAL^5 PHILLIPS (Villula Armelia^4 Moore, Robert Bennett^3 Moore I, Robert Marian^2 Moore, Zachariah^1 Moore) was born on 02 May 1916. She married BILL LANIER.
Bill Lanier and Opal PHILLIPS had the following child:

      i.   LEE^6 LANIER (son of Bill Lanier and Opal PHILLIPS).

44.   ARTHUR^5 PHILLIPS JR. (Villula Armelia^4 Moore, Robert Bennett^3 Moore I, Robert Marian^2 Moore, Zachariah^1 Moore). He married LENA HUDSON.
Arthur PHILLIPS Jr. and Lena Hudson had the following children:

100.   i.   JEAN^6 PHILLIPS (daughter of Arthur PHILLIPS Jr. and Lena Hudson). She married MAX BLACKMON.

101.   ii.   VIRGINIA LEE PHILLIPS (daughter of Arthur PHILLIPS Jr. and Lena Hudson). She married EMMETT LEE DOYLE.

45. **Coy B[5] Phillips** (Villula Armelia[4] Moore, Robert Bennett[3] Moore I, Robert Marian[2] Moore, Zachariah[1] Moore) was born in 1905 in Alabama, United States. He married **Adaline Mnu**.
Coy B PHILLIPS and Adaline MNU had the following child:

    i.   Bobby[6] Phillips (son of Coy B PHILLIPS and Adaline MNU).

46. **Roy C[5] Phillips** (Villula Armelia[4] Moore, Robert Bennett[3] Moore I, Robert Marian[2] Moore, Zachariah[1] Moore) was born in 1906 in Alabama, United States. He married **Mnu**.
Roy C PHILLIPS and MNU had the following children:

    i.   Roy[6] Phillips JR (son of Roy C PHILLIPS and MNU).

    ii.   Joan Phillips (daughter of Roy C PHILLIPS and MNU).

47. **Sara Pearl[5] Phillips** (Villula Armelia[4] Moore, Robert Bennett[3] Moore I, Robert Marian[2] Moore, Zachariah[1] Moore) was born on 04 Jul 1910 in Altoona, Etowah, Alabama, United States. She died on 22 Sep 1961 in Foley, Baldwin, Alabama, United States. She married **William Jordan Gulledge** on 22 Sep 1927 in Baldwin, Alabama, United States. He was born on 03 Jan 1905 in Rosinton, Alabama, United States. He died on 02 May 1990 in Robertsdale, Baldwin, Alabama, United States.

William Jordan GULLEDGE and Sara Pearl PHILLIPS had the following children:

    i.   Wesley[6] Gulledge (son of William Jordan GULLEDGE and Sara Pearl PHILLIPS).

    ii.   Betty Joe Gulledge (daughter of William Jordan GULLEDGE and Sara Pearl PHILLIPS).

    iii.   Dona Rita Gulledge (daughter of William Jordan GULLEDGE and Sara Pearl PHILLIPS) was born on 04 Dec 1931 in Robertsdale, Baldwin, Alabama, United States. She died on 01 Jun 2007 in Daphne, Baldwin, Alabama, United States.

48. **Grady Woodrow[5] Phillips** (Villula Armelia[4] Moore, Robert Bennett[3] Moore I, Robert Marian[2] Moore, Zachariah[1] Moore) was born on 16 May 1919 in Alabama, United States. He died on 20 Jul 2008 in Dallas, Dallas, Texas, United States. He married **Dorris Cockerham**.
Grady Woodrow PHILLIPS and Dorris Cockerham had the following children:

    i.   Woody[6] Phillips (son of Grady Woodrow PHILLIPS and Dorris Cockerham).

    ii.   Donna Phillips (daughter of Grady Woodrow PHILLIPS and Dorris Cockerham).

49. **Edwin Leon[5] Moore** (James Robert[4], Benjamin Martin[3], Robert Marian[2], Zachariah[1]) was born on 05 May 1906 in Union Point,AL. He married (1) **Gussie Rasco** on 17 Jul 1928. He married (3) **Gussie Rasco**.

Edwin Leon Moore and Gussie Rasco had the following children:

102.   ii.   Betty Jo Moore (daughter of Edwin Leon Moore and Gussie Rasco) was born on 3 Mar 1931. She married William Henry Ashley on 09 Jun 1951. He was born on 31 Jul 1925. He died on 16 Nov 2005.

103.   iii.   Dan Robert Moore (son of Edwin Leon Moore and Gussie Rasco) was born on 16 Mar 1934 in Oneonta,Alabama. He died on 19 Jun 1990 in Oneonta, Blount, Alabama (Burial Oak Hill Cemetery). He married Ann Hudson.

104.   iv.   Sallie Ann Moore (daughter of Edwin Leon Moore and Gussie Rasco). She married John Pitts.

50. **CLARA**[5] **BURNS** (Mary Ethel[4] Moore, Benjamin Martin[3] Moore, Robert Marian[2] Moore, Zachariah[1] Moore). She married **JOE B. GUNNELLS**.

Joe B. Gunnells and Clara Burns had the following child:

   i.   MARY EVELYN[6] GUNNELLS (daughter of Joe B. Gunnells and Clara Burns).

51. **JEROME J.**[5] **BURNS** (Mary Ethel[4] Moore, Benjamin Martin[3] Moore, Robert Marian[2] Moore, Zachariah[1] Moore). He married **EVELYN WHITE**.

Jerome J. Burns and Evelyn White had the following children:

   i.   WAYNE[6] BURNS (son of Jerome J. Burns and Evelyn White). He died in 1972.

106.   ii.   TOMMY BURNS (son of Jerome J. Burns and Evelyn White). He married BARBARA WIGGINS.

52. **MERLE**[5] **BURNS** (Mary Ethel[4] Moore, Benjamin Martin[3] Moore, Robert Marian[2] Moore, Zachariah[1] Moore). She married **WALTER MAJORS**.

Walter Majors and Merle Burns had the following children:

106.   i.   JANIE[6] MAJORS (daughter of Walter Majors and Merle Burns). She married DONALD GREY.

   ii.   CATHY MAJORS (daughter of Walter Majors and Merle Burns).

   iii.   AMY MAJORS (daughter of Walter Majors and Merle Burns).

53. **MAX**[5] **DAILEY** (Ola Frances[4] Moore, Benjamin Martin[3] Moore, Robert Marian[2] Moore, Zachariah[1] Moore). He married **JEAN INGRAM**.

Max Dailey and Jean Ingram had the following child:

   i.   DAILEY[6] MAX JR. (son of Max Dailey and Jean Ingram).

54. **RALPH MOORE**[5] **BYNUM** (Beulah Ennis[4] Moore, Benjamin Martin[3] Moore, Robert Marian[2] Moore, Zachariah[1] Moore). He married **SYBLE COLE**.

Ralph Moore Bynum and Syble Cole had the following children:

   i.   STANLEY DON[6] BYNUM (son of Ralph Moore Bynum and Syble Cole).

   ii.   MARCHIS BYNUM (daughter of Ralph Moore Bynum and Syble Cole). She married TOMMY LIMBAUGH.

   iii.   KATHERLEEN BYNUM (daughter of Ralph Moore Bynum and Syble Cole).

   iv.   CURTIS BYNUM (son of Ralph Moore Bynum and Syble Cole).

55. **RACHEL**[5] **BYNUM** (Beulah Ennis[4] Moore, Benjamin Martin[3] Moore, Robert Marian[2] Moore, Zachariah[1] Moore). She married **LUTHER BENTLEY JR.**.

Luther Bentley Jr. and Rachel Bynum had the following children:

   i.   DANNY[6] BENTLEY (son of Luther Bentley Jr. and Rachel Bynum). He married MARGARET MILLER.

108.   ii.   TERRY T. BENTLEY (daughter of Luther Bentley Jr. and Rachel Bynum). She married TOMMY LOWREY.

   iii.   DEBBIE D. BENTLEY (daughter of Luther Bentley Jr. and Rachel Bynum).

   iv.   JAMES R. BOB BENTLEY (son of Luther Bentley Jr. and Rachel Bynum).

   v.   MARY EMILIY BENTLEY (child of Luther Bentley Jr. and Rachel Bynum).

56.   **FANNIE NAN**[5] **BYNUM** (Beulah Ennis[4] Moore, Benjamin Martin[3] Moore, Robert Marian[2] Moore, Zachariah[1] Moore). She married **JOHNNY DAVIS**.

Johnny Davis and Fannie Nan Bynum had the following children:

  i.   JA NAN[6] DAVIS (daughter of Johnny Davis and Fannie Nan Bynum).

  ii.   DAVIS JOHNNY JR. (son of Johnny Davis and Fannie Nan Bynum).

57.   **CONSTANCE IVALEEN**[5] **MOORE** (Charles Claude[4], Dr. James "Jimmy" Hamilton[3] D.MD, Robert Marian[2], Zachariah[1]) was born on 13 Dec 1911 in Blount County, Alabama, USA. She died on 07 Nov 1993 in Oneonta, AL USA Buried in Marshall Memory Gardens, Marshall, Alabama, United States. She married **ZOLEN TRACY CURREY** on 26 Mar 1939 in Marshall County, Alabama, USA. He was born on 06 Oct 1905 in Marshall County, Alabama, USA. He died on 06 Oct 1995 in Oneonta, Blount, Alabama, USA.

Zolen Tracy Currey and Constance Ivaleen Moore had the following children:

  i.   RALPH TRACY[6] CURREY (son of Zolen Tracy Currey and Constance Ivaleen Moore) was born on 26 Mar 1940 in Blount County, Alabama, USA. He died on 24 Oct 2004 in Blount County, Alabama, USA.

109. ii.   CONSTANCE MARIE CURREY (daughter of Zolen Tracy Currey and Constance Ivaleen Moore) was born on 27 Jun 1944 in Birmingham, Jefferson, Alabama, USA. She married JERRY RUSSELL JACKSON on 08 Sep 1962. He was born on 05 Feb 1940 in Etowah, Alabama, USA.

58.   **LEILA REBECCA**[5] **MOORE** (Charles Claude[4], Dr. James "Jimmy" Hamilton[3] D.MD, Robert Marian[2], Zachariah[1]) was born on 13 Oct 1913 in Alabama. She died on 25 Mar 2001 in Antioch Church of Christ. She married **CONNIE HARLEY MILLER** on 17 Dec 1938. He was born on 22 Apr 1906.

Connie Harley Miller and Leila Rebecca Moore had the following children:

109. i.   ROY WESLEY[6] MILLER (son of Connie Harley Miller and Leila Rebecca Moore) was born on 05 Jan 1942. He married ELIZABETH ANN ELIAS. She was born on 16 Mar 1951.

110. ii.   GLEN CONNIE MILLER (son of Connie Harley Miller and Leila Rebecca Moore) was born on 06 Sep 1946. He married BARBARA ANN PINSON. She was born on 05 Jan 1948. She died on 14 Jun 1988 (Burial in Antioch Cemetery).

111. iii.   REBECCA ELAINE MILLER (daughter of Connie Harley Miller and Leila Rebecca Moore) was born on 27 Jul 1949. She married JOHNNY NELSON SISSON on 28 Jul 1967. He was born on 12 Sep 1948.

59.   **ADA ETHEL**[5] **MOORE** (Charles Claude[4], Dr. James "Jimmy" Hamilton[3] D.MD, Robert Marian[2], Zachariah[1]) was born on 28 Jun 1920 in Blount County. She married **CHARLES RENFRO ODEN**. He was born on 25 Apr 1919. He died on 01 Apr 2003.

Charles Renfro Oden and Ada Ethel Moore had the following children:

112. i.   JANET ROBERTA[6] ODEN (daughter of Charles Renfro Oden and Ada Ethel Moore) was born on 20 Dec 1944. She married JIMMY RODDAM. He was born on 23 Dec 1943.

113. ii.   CHARLES ODEN (son of Charles Renfro Oden and Ada Ethel Moore). He married GAYLE LEATHERWOOD.

60. **HENRY GRADY**[5] **HOLLAND** (Lula Ladora Dora[4] Moore, Dr. James "Jimmy" Hamilton[3] Moore D.MD, Robert Marian[2] Moore, Zachariah[1] Moore) was born on 20 Sep 1911 in Blount County, Alabama, USA. He died on 01 Aug 1992 in Gadsden, Etowah, Alabama, USA. He married **CLEO FREEMAN**. She was born on 28 Jan 1920 in Hamilton County, Tennessee, USA. She died on 23 Mar 2010 in Gadsden, Etowah, Alabama, USA.

    Henry Grady Holland and Cleo Freeman had the following children:

    114.   i.   INGA[6] HOLLAND (daughter of Henry Grady Holland and Cleo Freeman). She married DONNIE HANLEY.

            ii.   DONNA HOLLAND (daughter of Henry Grady Holland and Cleo Freeman).

61. **RAY KYTLE**[5] **HOLLAND SR.** (Lula Ladora Dora[4] Moore, Dr. James "Jimmy" Hamilton[3] Moore D.MD, Robert Marian[2] Moore, Zachariah[1] Moore) was born on 26 Sep 1912 in Alabama. He died on 29 Dec 1963 in Gadsden, Etowah, Alabama. He married **BART KELLY**. She was born on 15 Jun 1911 in Marshall County, Alabama, USA. She died on 08 Dec 2003 in Gadsden, Etowah, Alabama, USA.

    Ray Kytle Holland Sr. and Bart Kelly had the following children:

    115.   i.   GINGER[6] HOLLAND (daughter of Ray Kytle Holland Sr. and Bart Kelly). She married PAT BARKLEY.

    116.   ii.   RAY KYTLE HOLLAND JR. (son of Ray Kytle Holland Sr. and Bart Kelly). He married MYRA B KIRBY on 17 Jul 1985 in Clark, Nevada.

62. **JAMES B**[5] **HOLLAND** (Lula Ladora Dora[4] Moore, Dr. James "Jimmy" Hamilton[3] Moore D.MD, Robert Marian[2] Moore, Zachariah[1] Moore) was born about 1916 in Alabama. He married **FLORENCE BENZ**. James B Holland and Florence Benz had the following children:

            i.   SANDRA (ADOPTED)[6] HOLLAND (daughter of James B Holland and Florence Benz).

            ii.   MARGARET HOLLAND (daughter of James B Holland and Florence Benz). She married MAX MARTIN.

    118.   iii. MARIE HOLLAND (daughter of James B Holland and Florence Benz). She married DARTON SAYLOR.

    119.   iv.   ROBERT OLIVER HOLLAND (son of James B Holland and Florence Benz). He married DONNA CLARK.

63. **L SANDERS**[5] **HOLLAND** (Lula Ladora Dora[4] Moore, Dr. James "Jimmy" Hamilton[3] Moore D.MD, Robert Marian[2] Moore, Zachariah[1] Moore) was born about 1921 in Alabama. He married **GLADYS HARDER**.

    L Sanders Holland and Gladys Harder had the following children:

            i.   JENNIFER (ADOPTED)[6] HOLLAND (daughter of L Sanders Holland and Gladys Harder).

            ii.   CHRISTINE (ADOPTED) HOLLAND (daughter of L Sanders Holland and Gladys Harder).

64. **C AVONELL**[5] **HOLLAND** (Lula Ladora Dora[4] Moore, Dr. James "Jimmy" Hamilton[3] Moore D.MD, Robert Marian[2] Moore, Zachariah[1] Moore) was born about 1924 in Alabama. She married (2) **ROSS SMITH**.

    Ross Smith and C Avonell Holland had the following child:

    119.   i.   NEIL[6] SMITH (son of Ross Smith and C Avonell Holland). He married BETTY SCOTT.

65. **W EVERETT "PUG"^{5} HOLLAND** (Lula Ladora Dora^4 Moore, Dr. James "Jimmy" Hamilton^3 Moore D.MD, Robert Marian^2 Moore, Zachariah^1 Moore) was born about 1926 in Alabama. He married **LOIS ALLISON**.
    W Everett "Pug" Holland and Lois Allison had the following children:
    i. CRAIG^6 HOLLAND (son of W Everett "Pug" Holland and Lois Allison).
    ii. JEFFERY HOLLAND (son of W Everett "Pug" Holland and Lois Allison).
    iii. GLENN HOLLAND (son of W Everett "Pug" Holland and Lois Allison).
    iv. DORSEY HOLLAND (son of W Everett "Pug" Holland and Lois Allison).

66. **VALERIA^5 ELLER** (Susie Iola^4 Moore, Dr. James "Jimmy" Hamilton^3 Moore D.MD, Robert Marian^2 Moore, Zachariah^1 Moore) was born about 1916 in Alabama. She died on 13 Jul 1995 in Clayton, Georgia. She married **EUGENE OGLE**.

    Eugene Ogle and Valeria Eller had the following children:
    i. WAYNE^6 OGLE (son of Eugene Ogle and Valeria Eller).
    121. ii. HARVEY OGLE (son of Eugene Ogle and Valeria Eller). He married MNU.

67. **OSMOND^5 ELLER** (Susie Iola^4 Moore, Dr. James "Jimmy" Hamilton^3 Moore D.MD, Robert Marian^2 Moore, Zachariah^1 Moore) was born about 1919 in Alabama. He married **ALLENE ADAMSON**.
    Osmond Eller and Allene Adamson had the following child:
    i. SUSAN^6 ELLER (daughter of Osmond Eller and Allene Adamson).

68. **LILLIAN^5 ELLER** (Susie Iola^4 Moore, Dr. James "Jimmy" Hamilton^3 Moore D.MD, Robert Marian^2 Moore, Zachariah^1 Moore) was born about 1923 in Alabama. She married **GEORGE PRICHARD**.
    George Prichard and Lillian Eller had the following child:
    121. i. JUDY^6 PRICHARD (daughter of George Prichard and Lillian Eller). She married KITE.

69. **GRACE^5 ELLER** (Susie Iola^4 Moore, Dr. James "Jimmy" Hamilton^3 Moore D.MD, Robert Marian^2 Moore, Zachariah^1 Moore) was born in 1928 in Georgia. She married **ARTHUR BENEFIELD**, son of Oscar Benefield and Lillie Sorrells. He was born on 29 Sep 1925 in Decatur, Georgia. He died on 3 Nov 1994 in East Point, Fulton County, Georgia.

    Arthur Benefield and Grace Eller had the following children:
    i. RANDY^6 BENEFIELD (son of Arthur Benefield and Grace Eller).
    ii. ALAN BENEFIELD (son of Arthur Benefield and Grace Eller).
    122. iii. CATHY BENEFIELD (daughter of Arthur Benefield and Grace Eller). She married MIKE GADDIS.
    123. iv. ELAINE BENEFIELD (daughter of Arthur Benefield and Grace Eller). She married BOB BRYAN.

70. **JAMES CARL "JIMMY"^{5} MOORE** (James Carl^4, Dr. James "Jimmy" Hamilton^3 D.MD, Robert Marian^2, Zachariah^1) was born about 1929 in Alabama. He married **JANE BROCK**.
    James Carl "Jimmy" Moore and Jane Brock had the following child:
    i. TERESA^6 MOORE (child of James Carl "Jimmy" Moore and Jane Brock).

71. **ROBERT C. (BOB)**[5] **MOORE JR.** (Robert Cayce[4], Dr. James "Jimmy" Hamilton[3] D.MD, Robert Marian[2], Zachariah[1]) was born on 12 Jul 1946. He married **BETTY POSEY**. She was born on 20 Dec 1946.

Robert C. (Bob) Moore Jr. and Betty Posey had the following children:

124.   i.   BRADLEY ROBERT[6] MOORE (son of Robert C. (Bob) Moore Jr. and Betty Posey) was born on 01 May 1975. He married JENNIFER QUICK. She was born on 10 May 1974.

         ii.   BART SAMMY MOORE (son of Robert C. (Bob) Moore Jr. and Betty Posey) was born on 08 Jan 1977. He married LESLIE BORDEN. She was born on 07 Mar 1977.

72. **EARL OLIVER**[5] **MURRAY** (Adda Vesta[4] Moore, Daniel Marion[3] Moore, Robert Marian[2] Moore, Zachariah[1] Moore) was born on 02 Sep 1902 in Alabama. He died on 05 Feb 1972 in Birmingham, Jefferson, Alabama, United States of America. He married **A RTIE MAE LONG** on 06 Sep 1926 in Cherokee Co, AL. She was born on 15 Jan 1909 in Georgia. She died on 24 Mar 1970 in Birmingham, Jefferson, Alabama, United States of America.

Earl Oliver Murray and Artie Mae Long had the following child:

         i.   SHARON ANN[6] MURRAY (daughter of Earl Oliver Murray and Artie Mae Long). She married STEVEN SEVERY.

73. **THOMAS HERMAN**[5] **MURRAY** (Adda Vesta[4] Moore, Daniel Marion[3] Moore, Robert Marian[2] Moore, Zachariah[1] Moore) was born on 20 Jul 1908 in Alabama, USA. He died on 16 Sep 1984 in North Augusta, Aiken, South Carolina, United States of America. He married **MARY GLADYS CHAFFIN** on 18 Mar 1928 in Lawrence, Tennessee. She was born on 19 Mar 1907 in Tennessee. She died on 14 Nov 1987 in Charleston, Charleston, South Carolina, United States of America.

Thomas Herman Murray and Mary Gladys Chaffin had the following child:

125.   i.   HERMAN CLAY[6] MURRAY (son of Thomas Herman Murray and Mary Gladys Chaffin). He married PATRICIA GAIL DRAKE.

74. **CORNELIA IRENE**[5] **MURRAY** (Adda Vesta[4] Moore, Daniel Marion[3] Moore, Robert Marian[2] Moore, Zachariah[1] Moore) was born on 16 Jul 1919 in Alabama, USA. She died on 02 Jul 2011 in Germantown, Shelby, Tennessee, USA. She married **ARTHUR JAMES MARSON**.

Arthur James Marson and Cornelia Irene Murray had the following children:

126.   i.   ROBERT BRUCE[6] MARSON (son of Arthur James Marson and Cornelia Irene Murray) was born on 14 Dec 1945. He married LOIS JEAN RUSSELL.

127.   ii.   ALICE JEAN MARSON (daughter of Arthur James Marson and Cornelia Irene Murray) was born on 21 Aug 1948. She married RONALD F STEVENS.

         iii. PATRICHIA ANN MARSON (daughter of Arthur James Marson and Cornelia Irene Murray) was born on 28 Apr 1955.

75. **IMOGENE F**[5] **MOORE** (William Oscar[4], Daniel Marion[3], Robert Marian[2], Zachariah[1]) was born on 12 Aug 1917 in Alabama. She died on 21 Dec 1996 in Deatsville, Elmore, Alabama, United States of America. She married **JESSIE J WHITWORTH**. He was born on 28 Jun 1917. He died in Jun 1983 in Blountsville, Blount, Alabama, United States of America.

Jessie J Whitworth and Imogene F Moore had the following children:

         i.   JOHN RODNEY[6] WHITWORTH (son of Jessie J Whitworth and Imogene F Moore).

         ii.   JAMES OSCAR WHITWORTH (son of Jessie J Whitworth and Imogene F Moore). He married KAREN HERMON.

128.   iii.   JOE LYNN WHITWORTH (son of Jessie J Whitworth and Imogene F Moore). He married CAROL DAUGHTERY.

          iv.   ROBERT MOORE WHITWORTH (son of Jessie J Whitworth and Imogene F Moore). He married JANICE DUTTON.

          v.   RALPH MARLON WHITWORTH (son of Jessie J Whitworth and Imogene F Moore) was born on 28 Jul 1937 in Blount Co AL. He died on 03 Sep 1940.

          vi.   RAY HARLON WHITWORTH (son of Jessie J Whitworth and Imogene F Moore) was born on 11 Feb 1938 in Blount Co AL. He died on 16 Apr 1939 in Jefferson Co AL.

          vii.   DOROTHY IMOGENE WHITWORTH (daughter of Jessie J Whitworth and Imogene F Moore) was born in Blount Co., AL. She died in 2007 in Montgomery County, Alabama, USA. She married TED MCDANIEL.

129.   viii.   PHILLIP DALE WHITWORTH (son of Jessie J Whitworth and Imogene F Moore) was born. He died. He married VIRGIIA BROOKS.

76.   **V MAXINE⁵ MOORE** (William Oscar⁴, Daniel Marion³, Robert Marian², Zachariah¹) was born about 1922 in Alabama. He died on 20 Dec 2003 in Birmingham, Jefferson, Alabama, USA. He married **SYLVIA HIPP.**

V Maxine Moore and Sylvia Hipp had the following children:

          i.   DORA JANE⁶ MOORE (daughter of V Maxine Moore and Sylvia Hipp).

          ii.   HELEN CAROL HIPP (daughter of V Maxine Moore and Sylvia Hipp). She married JERRY HAMMOND.

130.   iii.   MICHAEL DOUGLASS HIPP (son of V Maxine Moore and Sylvia Hipp). He married ELLEN AYERS.

77.   **DORA J⁵ MOORE** (William Oscar⁴, Daniel Marion³, Robert Marian², Zachariah¹) was born about 1926 in Alabama. She married **JAMES C. HALLMARK.**

James C. Hallmark and Dora J Moore had the following children:

          i.   PATRICIA CAROL (ADOPTED)⁶ HALLMARK (daughter of James C. Hallmark and Dora J Moore).

          ii.   DONNA SUE (ADOPTED) HALLMARK (daughter of James C. Hallmark and Dora J Moore).

78.   **BARBARA ANN⁵ WHITE** (Vernice C.⁴ Moore, Daniel Marion³ Moore, Robert Marian² Moore, Zachariah¹ Moore). She married **ADOLPHOUS FREDERICK WILSON.**

Adolphous Frederick Wilson and Barbara Ann White had the following children:

          i.   BARBARA ANN⁶ WILSON (daughter of Adolphous Frederick Wilson and Barbara Ann White).

          ii.   ADOLPHUS FREDERICK WILSON JR. (son of Adolphous Frederick Wilson and Barbara Ann White).

79.   **LEWIS HERBON⁵ WHITE JR** (Vernice C.⁴ Moore, Daniel Marion³ Moore, Robert Marian² Moore, Zachariah¹ Moore) was born on 28 Nov 1923 in Alabama. He died on 18 Dec 1973 in Blountsville, Alabama, USA. He married **EVA YVONNE DOBSON.** She was born on 28 Feb 1927. She died on 05 Mar 2010 in Oxford, Alabama, USA.

Lewis Herbon White Jr and Eva Yvonne Dobson had the following children:

    i.   LARRY[6] WHITE (son of Lewis Herbon White Jr and Eva Yvonne Dobson).

    ii.   VICKEY WHITE (daughter of Lewis Herbon White Jr and Eva Yvonne Dobson).

    iii.   LINDA WHITE (daughter of Lewis Herbon White Jr and Eva Yvonne Dobson). She married JEAN SILAS.

132.   iv.   PAULETTE WHITE (daughter of Lewis Herbon White Jr and Eva Yvonne Dobson). She married HAROLD JOHNSON.

80.   **RUBY J[5] WHITE** (Vernice C.[4] Moore, Daniel Marion[3] Moore, Robert Marian[2] Moore, Zachariah[1] Moore) was born about 1928 in Alabama. She married **JOE BAIN MARTIN**.

Joe Bain Martin and Ruby J White had the following child:

    i.   ANN MARIE[6] MARTIN (daughter of Joe Bain Martin and Ruby J White).

81.   **ARNELL E[5] MOORE** (Robert Bennett[4] II, Daniel Marion[3], Robert Marian[2], Zachariah[1]) was born about 1924 in Alabama. He married **MILDRED NIBBLET**.

Arnell E Moore and Mildred Nibblet had the following children:

    i.   BETTY GALE[6] MOORE (daughter of Arnell E Moore and Mildred Nibblet).

132.   ii.   NELIA SUE MOORE (daughter of Arnell E Moore and Mildred Nibblet). She married UKN.

82.   **WONDALINE[5] MOORE** (Robert Bennett[4] II, Daniel Marion[3], Robert Marian[2], Zachariah[1]) was born about 1926 in Alabama. She married **GERALD RIDGEWAY**.

Gerald Ridgeway and Wondaline Moore had the following child:

    i.   LARRY G.[6] RIDGEWAY (son of Gerald Ridgeway and Wondaline Moore) was born on 26 Jul 1948. He married MARGO THOMAS.

83.   **ATTICE LOLA[5] HARVEY** (Dona Pearl Donie[4] Adams, Nancy A Elizabeth[3] Moore, Robert Marian[2] Moore, Zachariah[1] Moore) was born on 16 Apr 1910 in Blount, Alabama, USA. She died on 21 Jul 1969 in Altoona, Etowah, Alabama, USA. She married **CONNIE MACK SHELTON**. He was born on 22 Dec 1910 in Brooksville, Blount, Alabama, USA. He died on 08 Dec 1961 in Cullman, Cullman, Alabama.

Connie Mack Shelton and Attice Lola Harvey had the following child:

133.   i.   HARVEY LEE[6] SHELTON (son of Connie Mack Shelton and Attice Lola Harvey). He married DELORES PULLEN.

84.   **BRADY CORDELL[5] HARVEY** (Dona Pearl Donie[4] Adams, Nancy A Elizabeth[3] Moore, Robert Marian[2] Moore, Zachariah[1] Moore) was born on 02 May 1911 in Blount, Alabama, USA. He died on 15 Jan 2006 in Altoona, Etowah, Alabama, USA. He married **BERNICE WAID** on 23 Dec 1932. She was born on 23 Aug 1912 in Blountsville, Blount, AL, USA. She died on 02 Jun 1998 in Altoona, Etowah, AL.

Brady Cordell Harvey and Bernice Waid had the following child:

134.   i.   JAMES CORDELL[6] HARVEY (son of Brady Cordell Harvey and Bernice Waid). He married SHIRLEY SOUTHERN.

85.   **Spud Earl**[5] **Adams** (Napoleon Eugene[4], Nancy A Elizabeth[3] Moore, Robert Marian[2] Moore, Zachariah[1] Moore) was born about 1914 in Alabama. He married **Maurine Talton**.
      Spud Earl Adams and Maurine Talton had the following children:
      135.   i.   James Earl[6] Adams (son of Spud Earl Adams and Maurine Talton).
      136.   ii.   Joann Adams (daughter of Spud Earl Adams and Maurine Talton). She married L.D. Corbell.

86.   **Lydoth**[5] **Adams** (Napoleon Eugene[4], Nancy A Elizabeth[3] Moore, Robert Marian[2] Moore, Zachariah[1] Moore) was born about 1920 in Alabama. She married **Douglass Steffanauer**.
      Douglass Steffanauer and Lydoth Adams had the following children:
             i.   David Wayne "butch"[6] Steffanauer (son of Douglass Steffanauer and Lydoth Adams).
             ii.   Danny Steffanauer (son of Douglass Steffanauer and Lydoth Adams). He married Judy Young.
      137.   iii. Douglass Steffanauer Jr. (son of Douglass Steffanauer and Lydoth Adams). He married Julie Cunningham.

87.   **Gussie Lewis**[5] **Adams** (Laborn Elijah[4], Nancy A Elizabeth[3] Moore, Robert Marian[2] Moore, Zachariah[1] Moore) was born on 05 Sep 1904 in Susan Moore, Blount, Alabama, United States. He died on 08 Nov 1995 in Arab, Marshall, Alabama, United States. He married **Annie Ruby Jones**. She was born on 14 Aug 1924 in Brooksville, Blount, Alabama, United States. She died on 19 Feb 2004 in Arab, Marshall, Alabama, United States.

      Gussie Lewis Adams and Annie Ruby Jones had the following children:
      138.   i.   Betty Fay[6] Adams (daughter of Gussie Lewis Adams and Annie Ruby Jones). She married John L. Larue.
      139.   ii.   Gladys Adams (daughter of Gussie Lewis Adams and Annie Ruby Jones). She married Oliver J. Smith.
             iii. Eugene Walker Adams (son of Gussie Lewis Adams and Annie Ruby Jones) was born on 08 Jun 1935 in Brooksville, Blount, Alabama, United States. He died on 19 Mar 1946 in Brooksville, Blount, Alabama, United States.
      140.   iv.   Fred Jackson Adams (son of Gussie Lewis Adams and Annie Ruby Jones) was born on 20 Apr 1937 in Brooksville, Blount, Alabama, United States. He died on 15 Apr 1976 in Arab, Marshall, Alabama, United States of America. He married Ruth Thompson.
      141.   v.   Maxie Sue Adams (daughter of Gussie Lewis Adams and Annie Ruby Jones). She married Jack L. Rigsby.
      142.   vi.   Donald L. Adams (son of Gussie Lewis Adams and Annie Ruby Jones). He married Verlie M. Laten.

88.   **Aldie**[5] **Adams** (Laborn Elijah[4], Nancy A Elizabeth[3] Moore, Robert Marian[2] Moore, Zachariah[1] Moore) was born in 1908 in Alabama, United States. He died on 26 Jun 1981 in Ashtabula County, Ohio, USA. He married **L Ethel Hill**. She was born about 1909 in Alabama.

Aldie Adams and L Ethel Hill had the following children:

        i.   LYNN[6] ADAMS (son of Aldie Adams and L Ethel Hill). He married MARGARET MNU.

143.   ii.   JIMMY ADAMS (son of Aldie Adams and L Ethel Hill). He married LILLIAN MNU.

144.   iii. BARBARA ADAMS (daughter of Aldie Adams and L Ethel Hill). She married CLIFFORD MASON.

145.   iv. BILLY ADAMS (son of Aldie Adams and L Ethel Hill). He married DORIS REEVES.

146.   v.   HOYT E ADAMS (son of Aldie Adams and L Ethel Hill) was born about 1928 in Alabama. He married RUBY J. NIX.

147.   vi. MAVIS G ADAMS (daughter of Aldie Adams and L Ethel Hill) was born about 1930 in Alabama. She married HUBERT SMITH.

89.   ELLIS[5] ADAMS (Laborn Elijah[4], Nancy A Elizabeth[3] Moore, Robert Marian[2] Moore, Zachariah[1] Moore) was born in 1910 in Alabama, United States. He died in Jun 1983 in Horton, Marshall, Alabama, United States of America. He married (1) ANDERSON. He married (2) EUNICE SLOMAN. She was born about 1903 in Alabama.

Ellis Adams and Eunice Sloman had the following children:

148.   i.   JAMES E[6] ADAMS (son of Ellis Adams and Eunice Sloman) was born about 1930 in Alabama. He married LILLMA YANCEY.

149.   ii.   MARGARET ADAMS (daughter of Ellis Adams and Eunice Sloman). She married BUCK WEBB.

150.   iii. BOBBIE JEANETTE ADAMS (daughter of Ellis Adams and Eunice Sloman) was born on 31 Jan 1932 in Alabama. She died on 06 Sep 2001 in Alabama. She married HERBERT STEVENSON. He was born on 01 Jul 1925 in Alabama, USA. He died on 13 Jan 1993 in Alabama.

        iv. JAMES ADAMS (son of Ellis Adams and Eunice Sloman).

90.   MACK[5] ADAMS (Laborn Elijah[4], Nancy A Elizabeth[3] Moore, Robert Marian[2] Moore, Zachariah[1] Moore) was born on 15 Apr 1911 in Brooksville, Blount, Alabama, United States. He died on 15 Feb 1994 in Oneonta, Blount, Alabama, United States. He married ILA BEATRICE DOYLE on 20 Apr 1929 in Blount, Alabama, United States. She was born on 08 Aug 1909 in Brooksville, Blount, Alabama, United States. She died on 06 Nov 1991 in Birmingham, Jefferson, Alabama, United States.

Mack Adams and Ila Beatrice Doyle had the following children:

151.   i.   PATRICIA GAIL[6] ADAMS (daughter of Mack Adams and Ila Beatrice Doyle). She married JAMES T. WARD.

152.   ii.   GAYNELL ADAMS (daughter of Mack Adams and Ila Beatrice Doyle). She married (1) JERRY WARNICK. She married (2) JAMES H. FLACK.

153.   iii. JOHNNY MAC ADAMS (son of Mack Adams and Ila Beatrice Doyle). He married BARBARA ATCHLEY.

154.   iv. LUCILLE A DAMS (daughter of Mack Adams and Ila Beatrice Doyle). She married L. HERRING.

155.   v.   EVELYN A DAMS (daughter of Mack Adams and Ila Beatrice Doyle). She married JACK OSBORN.

91. LENA[5] ADAMS (Laborn Elijah[4], Nancy A Elizabeth[3] Moore, Robert Marian[2] Moore, Zachariah[1] Moore) was born about 1915 in Alabama. She married DELBERT BESHEARS, son of WILLIE WILKS BESHEARS and LUCY j KERR. He was born in Aug 1914 in Blount County, Alabama, USA. He died on 14 Apr 1984 in Gadsden, Alabama, USA.

Delbert Beshears and Lena Adams had the following children:

    156.   i.   VIRGINIA[6] BESHEARS (daughter of Delbert Beshears and Lena Adams). She married TOM BATES.

             ii.   ROGER BESHEARS (son of Delbert Beshears and Lena Adams). He married HENDRIX.

    157.   iii.   CHARLES BESHEARS (son of Delbert Beshears and Lena Adams). He married NONA MURPHREE.

    158.   iv.   MAGGIE BESHEARS (daughter of Delbert Beshears and Lena Adams). She married (1) BOBBY PATTERNSON. She married (2) RAY DUPREE.

    159.   v.   SUE BESHEARS (daughter of Delbert Beshears and Lena Adams). She married BILL STEWART.

    160.   vi.   RUTH BESHEARS (daughter of Delbert Beshears and Lena Adams). She married JUNIOR SNELL.

92. V JO[5] ADAMS (Laborn Elijah[4], Nancy A Elizabeth[3] Moore, Robert Marian[2] Moore, Zachariah[1] Moore) was born about 1918 in Alabama. She married HENRY BROWN.

Henry Brown and V Jo Adams had the following child:

    161.   i.   NADINE[6] BROWN (daughter of Henry Brown and V Jo Adams). She married BOBBY LAMB.

93. RECTOR[5] ADAMS (Laborn Elijah[4], Nancy A Elizabeth[3] Moore, Robert Marian[2] Moore, Zachariah[1] Moore) was born in 1920 in Alabama. He died in 2008. He married EVE MARTIS.

Rector Adams and Eve Martis had the following children:

    162.   i.   JAMES[6] ADAMS (son of Rector Adams and Eve Martis). He married MARY LARUE.

    163.   ii.   KENNETH ADAMS (son of Rector Adams and Eve Martis). He married GAIL ROSCOE.

             iii.   MICHAEL ADAMS (son of Rector Adams and Eve Martis).

             iv.   RAYMOND ADAMS (son of Rector Adams and Eve Martis).

94. C PEARL[5] ADAMS (Laborn Elijah[4], Nancy A Elizabeth[3] Moore, Robert Marian[2] Moore, Zachariah[1] Moore) was born about 1924 in Alabama. She married TEAGUE.

Teague and C Pearl Adams had the following children:

    164.   i.   COLEMAN[6] TEAGUE (son of Teague and C Pearl Adams). He married BETTY J SNELL.

    165.   ii.   FRANCES TEAGUE (daughter of Teague and C Pearl Adams). She married JAMES BULLARD.

95. EULAS FLARE[5] BARNES (Sally Emmer Abagel[4] Adams, Nancy A Elizabeth[3] Moore, Robert Marian[2] Moore, Zachariah[1] Moore) was born on 05 Feb 1909 in Clarence, Blount, Alabama, USA. He died on 18 Apr 1990 in Pinson, Alabama, USA. He married IRENE SIMMONS. She was born on 07 Sep 1910 in Pinson, Alabama, USA. She died on 19 Aug 1998 in Pinson, Alabama, USA.

Eulas Flare Barnes and Irene Simmons had the following child:

166.   i.   CAROLYN[6] BARNES (daughter of Eulas Flare Barnes and Irene Simmons). She married WILLIAM THOMPSON.

96.   PLUMIE[5] BARNES (Sally Emmer Abagel[4] Adams, Nancy A Elizabeth[3] Moore, Robert Marian[2] Moore, Zachariah[1] Moore) was born on 06 Sep 1910 in Blount County, Alabama, USA. She died on 02 Jul 2010 in Birmingham, Jefferson, Alabama, USA. She married GEORGE HUSTON BESHEARS in 1928. He was born on 20 Jul 1911 in Alabama. He died on 06 Jul 1992 in Gadsden, Alabama. George Huston Beshears and Plumie Barnes had the following children:

167.   i.   S. W.[6] BESHEARS (child of George Huston Beshears and Plumie Barnes) was born about 1930 in Alabama. He married HARRIET SOLTER.

168.   ii. DOROTHY SUE BESHEARS (daughter of George Huston Beshears and Plumie Barnes) was born on 24 Jan 1931. She died on 06 Feb 1996 in Gadsden, Etowah, Alabama, United States of America. She married (1) EASLEY KIRBY. She married (2) JIMMY CRUMP. She married (3) JOHN P PHILLIPS on 14 Sep 1963 in Gadsden, Etowah, Alabama, United States of America. He was born on 27 Nov 1918. He died on 23 Apr 2007 in Gadsden, Etowah, Alabama, United States of America.

97.   OREN E[5] BARNES (Sally Emmer Abagel[4] Adams, Nancy A Elizabeth[3] Moore, Robert Marian[2] Moore, Zachariah[1] Moore) was born on 07 Jun 1922 in Clarence, Blount, Alabama, USA. He died on 22 Oct 1977 in Birmingham, Jefferson, Alabama, USA. He married ZIZ BLAIR.

Oren E Barnes and Ziz Blair had the following children:

169.   i.   CHARLOTTE ANN[6] BARNES (daughter of Oren E Barnes and Ziz Blair). She married FRANK MOOTY.

        ii. DANNY BARNES (son of Oren E Barnes and Ziz Blair).

98.   MARY LOU[5] BARNES (Sally Emmer Abagel[4] Adams, Nancy A Elizabeth[3] Moore, Robert Marian[2] Moore, Zachariah[1] Moore) was born on 29 Aug 1928 in Clarence, Blount, Alabama, USA. She died on 12 May 2010 in Gadsden, Etowah, Alabama, United States of America. She married HERBERT BUICE.

Herbert Buice and Mary Lou Barnes had the following children:

        i.   DAVID[6] BUICE (son of Herbert Buice and Mary Lou Barnes).

        ii. LINDA BUICE (daughter of Herbert Buice and Mary Lou Barnes).

        iii. LA GAIL BUICE (daughter of Herbert Buice and Mary Lou Barnes).

Generation 6

99.   WILLIAM "BILLY" MOORE[6] MARTIN (Etoile E[5] Moore, William (Gus) Augustus[4] Moore, Robert Bennett[3] Moore I, Robert Marian[2] Moore, Zachariah[1] Moore). He married (1) LUCILLE WHITED. He married (2) GERTHA BEASELY.

William "Billy" Moore Martin and Lucille Whited had the following children:

        i.   JAMES D.[7] MARTIN (son of William "Billy" Moore Martin and Lucille Whited).

        ii. DONALD P. MARTIN (son of William "Billy" Moore Martin and Lucille Whited).

100. JEAN[6] PHILLIPS (Arthur[5] Jr., Villula Armelia[4] Moore, Robert Bennett[3] Moore I, Robert Marian[2] Moore, Zachariah[1] Moore). She married **MAX BLACKMON**.
      Max Blackmon and Jean PHILLIPS had the following child:
          i.   SCOTT[7] BLACKMON (son of Max Blackmon and Jean PHILLIPS).

101. VIRGINIA LEE[6] PHILLIPS (Arthur[5] Jr., Villula Armelia[4] Moore, Robert Bennett[3] Moore I, Robert Marian[2] Moore, Zachariah[1] Moore). She married **EMMETT LEE DOYLE**.
      Emmett Lee Doyle and Virginia Lee PHILLIPS had the following child:
          i.   PHILLIP LEE[7] DOYLE (son of Emmett Lee Doyle and Virginia Lee PHILLIPS).

102. BETTY JO[6] MOORE (Edwin Leon[5], James Robert[4], Benjamin Martin[3], Robert Marian[2], Zachariah[1]) was born on 03 Mar 1931. She married **WILLIAM HENRY ASHLEY** on 09 Jun 1951. He was born on 31 Jul 1925. He died on 16 Nov 2005.

      William Henry Ashley and Betty Jo Moore had the following children:
          i.   ANITA ASHLEY[7] MAY (daughter of William Henry Ashley and Betty Jo Moore) was born on 07 Jul 1953.
      171.   ii. VICKI ASHLEY BAURAIN (daughter of William Henry Ashley and Betty Jo Moore) was born on 26 Apr 1956.

103. DAN ROBERT[6] MOORE (Edwin Leon[5], James Robert[4], Benjamin Martin[3], Robert Marian[2], Zachariah[1]) was born on 16 Mar 1934 in Oneonta, Alabama. He died on 19 Jun 1990 in Oneonta, Blount, Alabama (Burial Oak Hill Cemetery). He married **ANN HUDSON**.

      Dan Robert Moore and Ann Hudson had the following children:
      172.   i. DANA[7] MOORE (daughter of Dan Robert Moore and Ann Hudson) was born in 1957. She married STEVE LANGFORD.
      173.   ii. MIKE MOORE (son of Dan Robert Moore and Ann Hudson) was born in 1959. He married NOT NAMED.
      174.   iii. MATT MOORE (son of Dan Robert Moore and Ann Hudson) was born in 1962. He married TAMMY SAUNDERS.

104. SALLIE ANN[6] MOORE (Edwin Leon[5], James Robert[4], Benjamin Martin[3], Robert Marian[2], Zachariah[1]). She married **JOHN PITTS**.
      John Pitts and Sallie Ann Moore had the following children:
          i.   JOY[7] PITTS (daughter of John Pitts and Sallie Ann Moore).
          ii. KIM PITTS (daughter of John Pitts and Sallie Ann Moore).
          iii. KAY PITTS (daughter of John Pitts and Sallie Ann Moore).

105. TOMMY[6] BURNS (Jerome J.[5], Mary Ethel[4] Moore, Benjamin Martin[3] Moore, Robert Marian[2] Moore, Zachariah[1] Moore). He married **BARBARA WIGGINS**.
      Tommy Burns and Barbara Wiggins had the following child:
          i.   DENISE[7] BURNS (daughter of Tommy Burns and Barbara Wiggins).

106.	JANIE[6] MAJORS (Merle[5] Burns, Mary Ethel[4] Moore, Benjamin Martin[3] Moore, Robert Marian[2] Moore, Zachariah[1] Moore). She married DONALD GREY.

Donald Grey and Janie Majors had the following children:

    i.   JEFFERY[7] GREY (son of Donald Grey and Janie Majors).

    ii.   ANTHONY GREY (son of Donald Grey and Janie Majors).

107.	TERRY T.[6] BENTLEY (Rachel[5] Bynum, Beulah Ennis[4] Moore, Benjamin Martin[3] Moore, Robert Marian[2] Moore, Zachariah[1] Moore). She married TOMMY LOWREY.

Tommy Lowrey and Terry T. Bentley had the following child:

    i.   BETSY[7] LOWREY (daughter of Tommy Lowrey and Terry T. Bentley).

108.	CONSTANCE MARIE[6] CURREY (Constance Ivaleen[5] Moore, Charles Claude[4] Moore, Dr. James "Jimmy" Hamilton[3] Moore D.MD, Robert Marian[2] Moore, Zachariah[1] Moore) was born on 27 Jun 1944 in Birmingham, Jefferson, Alabama, USA. She married JERRY RUSSELL JACKSON on 08 Sep 1962. He was born on 05 Feb 1940 in Etowah, Alabama, USA.

Jerry Russell Jackson and Constance Marie Currey had the following children:

175.	i. ALAN RUSSELL[7] JACKSON (son of Jerry Russell Jackson and Constance Marie Currey) was born on 01 Nov 1966 in Oneonta, Blount, Alabama, USA. He married TERESA VAN WAGNER. She was born in Mar 1971.

176.	ii. SCOTT CHRISTOPHER JACKSON (son of Jerry Russell Jackson and Constance Marie Currey) was born on 01 Feb 1971 in Oneonta, Blount, Alabama, USA. He married (1) MONICA SUZANNE MYRICK on 04 Nov 1990 in Snead, Blount, Alabama, USA (Bethel Baptist Church). She was born on 11 Jul 1973. He married (2) JULIA REBECCA DENISE EVANS on 01 Sep 2002 in Oneonta, Blount, Alabama, USA. She was born on 19 Apr 1975.

177.	iii. JASON ERIC JACKSON (son of Jerry Russell Jackson and Constance Marie Currey) was born on 21 Oct 1975 in Etowah, Gadsden, AL US. He married JAMI ALLYSON WEIR on 19 Dec 1998 in Gatlinburg, Sevier, Tennessee, USA. She was born on 27 Aug 1977.

109.	ROY WESLEY[6] MILLER (Leila Rebecca[5] Moore, Charles Claude[4] Moore, Dr. James "Jimmy" Hamilton[3] Moore D.MD, Robert Marian[2] Moore, Zachariah[1] Moore) was born on 05 Jan 1942. He married ELIZABETH ANN ELIAS. She was born on 16 Mar 1951.

Roy Wesley Miller and Elizabeth Ann Elias had the following children:

    i.   JOHN WESLEY[7] MILLER (son of Roy Wesley Miller and Elizabeth Ann Elias) was born on 21 Oct 1981.

    ii.   MATTHEW ROBERT MILLER (son of Roy Wesley Miller and Elizabeth Ann Elias) was born on 12 Feb 1987.

110.	GLEN CONNIE[6] MILLER (Leila Rebecca[5] Moore, Charles Claude[4] Moore, Dr. James "Jimmy" Hamilton[3] Moore D.MD, Robert Marian[2] Moore, Zachariah[1] Moore) was born on 06 Sep 1946. He married BARBARA ANN PINSON. She was born on 05 Jan 1948. She died on 14 Jun 1988 (Burial in Antioch Cemetery).

Glen Connie Miller and Barbara Ann Pinson had the following child:

    i.   WENDY MICHELLE[7] MILLER (daughter of Glen Connie Miller and Barbara Ann Pinson) was born on 26 Feb 1970. She died on 16 Mar 1991 in Died in Car Accident (Burial in Antioch Cemetery).

111.   **REBECCA ELAINE**[6] **MILLER** (Leila Rebecca[5] Moore, Charles Claude[4] Moore, Dr. James "Jimmy" Hamilton[3] Moore D.MD, Robert Marian[2] Moore, Zachariah[1] Moore) was born on 27 Jul 1949. She married **JOHNNY NELSON SISSON** on 28 Jul 1967. He was born on 12 Sep 1948.

Johnny Nelson Sisson and Rebecca Elaine Miller had the following child:

178.   i.   JOHN KEVIN[7] SISSON (son of Johnny Nelson Sisson and Rebecca Elaine Miller) was born on 26 Jan 1971. He married JILL GARDNER on 02 Sep 1994. She was born on 07 Mar 1973.

112.   **JANET ROBERTA**[6] **ODEN** (Ada Ethel[5] Moore, Charles Claude[4] Moore, Dr. James "Jimmy" Hamilton[3] Moore D.MD, Robert Marian[2] Moore, Zachariah[1] Moore) was born on 20 Dec 1944. She married **JIMMY RODDAM**. He was born on 23 Dec 1943.

Jimmy Roddam and Janet Roberta Oden had the following children:

179.   i.   MARK[7] RODDAM (son of Jimmy Roddam and Janet Roberta Oden). He married TAMMY DALE on 21 Apr 1990.

    ii.   KEITH RODDAM (son of Jimmy Roddam and Janet Roberta Oden) was born on 02 Oct 1972. He married CYNDI THATENHURST on 24 Apr 1999.

180.   iii.   LISA RODDAM (daughter of Jimmy Roddam and Janet Roberta Oden) was born on 24 May 1978. She married (1) ERIC MANDELL on 21 Nov 1998. She married (2) CHRIS JOHNSON on 10 Jun 2006. He was born on 02 Apr 1971.

113.   **CHARLES**[6] **ODEN** (Ada Ethel[5] Moore, Charles Claude[4] Moore, Dr. James "Jimmy" Hamilton[3] Moore D.MD, Robert Marian[2] Moore, Zachariah[1] Moore). He married **GAYLE LEATHERWOOD**.

Charles Oden and Gayle Leatherwood had the following children:

    i.   WESLEY[7] ODEN (son of Charles Oden and Gayle Leatherwood). He married EMILY MNU ODEN.

    ii.   JEREMY ODEN (son of Charles Oden and Gayle Leatherwood).

114.   **INGA**[6] **HOLLAND** (Henry Grady[5], Lula Ladora Dora[4] Moore, Dr. James "Jimmy" Hamilton[3] Moore D.MD, Robert Marian[2] Moore, Zachariah[1] Moore). She married **DONNIE HANLEY**.

Donnie Hanley and Inga Holland had the following child:

    i.   TRACY[7] HANLEY (daughter of Donnie Hanley and Inga Holland).

115.   **GINGER**[6] **HOLLAND** (Ray Kytle[5] Sr., Lula Ladora Dora[4] Moore, Dr. James "Jimmy" Hamilton[3] Moore D.MD, Robert Marian[2] Moore, Zachariah[1] Moore). She married **PAT BARKLEY**.

Pat Barkley and Ginger Holland had the following children:

    i.   TRICIA[7] HOLLAND (daughter of Pat Barkley and Ginger Holland).

    ii.   LANICE BARKLEY (daughter of Pat Barkley and Ginger Holland).

116. **RAY KYTLE**[6] **HOLLAND JR.** (Ray Kytle[5] Sr., Lula Ladora Dora[4] Moore, Dr. James "Jimmy" Hamilton[3] Moore D.MD, Robert Marian[2] Moore, Zachariah[1] Moore). He married **MYRA B KIRBY** on 17 Jul 1985 in Clark, Nevada.

Ray Kytle Holland Jr. and Myra B Kirby had the following child:

      i.   PAMELA[7] HOLLAND (daughter of Ray Kytle Holland Jr. and Myra B Kirby).

117. **MARIE**[6] **HOLLAND** (James B[5], Lula Ladora Dora[4] Moore, Dr. James "Jimmy" Hamilton[3] Moore D.MD, Robert Marian[2] Moore, Zachariah[1] Moore). She married **DARTON SAYLOR**.

Darton Saylor and Marie Holland had the following child:

      i.   JAMES C.[7] SAYLOR (son of Darton Saylor and Marie Holland).

118. **ROBERT OLIVER**[6] **HOLLAND** (James B[5], Lula Ladora Dora[4] Moore, Dr. James "Jimmy" Hamilton[3] Moore D.MD, Robert Marian[2] Moore, Zachariah[1] Moore). He married **DONNA CLARK**.

Robert Oliver Holland and Donna Clark had the following child:

      i.   PAUL DOUGLAS[7] HOLLAND (son of Robert Oliver Holland and Donna Clark).

119. **NEIL**[6] **SMITH** (C Avonell[5] Holland, Lula Ladora Dora[4] Moore, Dr. James "Jimmy" Hamilton[3] Moore D.MD, Robert Marian[2] Moore, Zachariah[1] Moore). He married **BETTY SCOTT**.

Neil Smith and Betty Scott had the following child:

      i.   MICHAEL[7] SMITH (son of Neil Smith and Betty Scott).

120. **HARVEY**[6] **OGLE** (Valeria[5] Eller, Susie Iola[4] Moore, Dr. James "Jimmy" Hamilton[3] Moore D.MD, Robert Marian[2] Moore, Zachariah[1] Moore). He married **MNU**.

Harvey Ogle and MNU had the following children:

      i.   TRACY[7] OGLE (daughter of Harvey Ogle and MNU).

      ii.   KIMBERLY OGLE (daughter of Harvey Ogle and MNU).

      iii. LANCE OGLE (son of Harvey Ogle and MNU).

121. **JUDY**[6] **PRICHARD** (Lillian[5] Eller, Susie Iola[4] Moore, Dr. James "Jimmy" Hamilton[3] Moore D.MD, Robert Marian[2] Moore, Zachariah[1] Moore). She married **KITE**.

Kite and Judy Prichard had the following children:

      i.   MICHAEL[7] KITE (son of Kite and Judy Prichard).

      ii.   JEFF KITE (son of Kite and Judy Prichard).

122. **CATHY**[6] **BENEFIELD** (Grace[5] Eller, Susie Iola[4] Moore, Dr. James "Jimmy" Hamilton[3] Moore D.MD, Robert Marian[2] Moore, Zachariah[1] Moore). She married **MIKE GADDIS**.

Mike Gaddis and Cathy Benefield had the following child:

      i.   MATT[7] GADDIS (son of Mike Gaddis and Cathy Benefield).

123. **ELAINE**[6] **BENEFIELD** (Grace[5] Eller, Susie Iola[4] Moore, Dr. James "Jimmy" Hamilton[3] Moore D.MD, Robert Marian[2] Moore, Zachariah[1] Moore). She married **BOB BRYAN**.

Bob Bryan and Elaine Benefield had the following children:

      i.   JASON[7] BRYAN (son of Bob Bryan and Elaine Benefield).

      ii.   AMY BRYAN (daughter of Bob Bryan and Elaine Benefield).

124. **BRADLEY ROBERT[6] MOORE** (Robert C. (Bob)[5] Jr., Robert Cayce[4], Dr. James "Jimmy" Hamilton[3] D.MD, Robert Marian[2], Zachariah[1]) was born on 01 May 1975. He married **JENNIFER QUICK**. She was born on 10 May 1974.

Bradley Robert Moore and Jennifer Quick had the following children:
   i.   MIKAH DOOLEY[7] (STEP) (daughter of Bradley Robert Moore and Jennifer Quick) was born on 22 Dec 1993.
   ii. MASON WILLIAMS (STEP) (son of Bradley Robert Moore and Jennifer Quick) was born on 09 Mar 1999.
   iii. SIDNEY WILLIAMS (STEP) (daughter of Bradley Robert Moore and Jennifer Quick) was born on 22 Jun 2001.

125. **HERMAN CLAY[6] MURRAY** (Thomas Herman[5], Adda Vesta[4] Moore, Daniel Marion[3] Moore, Robert Marian[2] Moore, Zachariah[1] Moore). He married **PATRICIA GAIL DRAKE**.
Herman Clay Murray and Patricia Gail Drake had the following children:
   i.   ROBERT CHAFFIN[7] MURRAY (son of Herman Clay Murray and Patricia Gail Drake) was born on 29 Oct 1937 in Birmingham, Jefferson, Alabama, USA. He died on 25 Sep 1995 in Fort Myers, Lee, Florida, United States of America.
   ii. JANET ANN MURRAY (daughter of Herman Clay Murray and Patricia Gail Drake).

126. **ROBERT BRUCE[6] MARSON** (Cornelia Irene[5] Murray, Adda Vesta[4] Moore, Daniel Marion[3] Moore, Robert Marian[2] Moore, Zachariah[1] Moore) was born on 14 Dec 1945. He married **LOIS JEAN RUSSELL**.
Robert Bruce Marson and Lois Jean Russell had the following children:
   i.   FLEETA MARIE[7] MARSON (daughter of Robert Bruce Marson and Lois Jean Russell).
   ii. ROBERT BRUCE MARSON JR. (son of Robert Bruce Marson and Lois Jean Russell).

127. **ALICE JEAN[6] MARSON** (Cornelia Irene[5] Murray, Adda Vesta[4] Moore, Daniel Marion[3] Moore, Robert Marian[2] Moore, Zachariah[1] Moore) was born on 21 Aug 1948. She married **RONALD F STEVENS**.
Ronald F Stevens and Alice Jean Marson had the following children:
   i.   ELIZABETH ASHLEY[7] STEVENS (daughter of Ronald F Stevens and Alice Jean Marson).
   ii. LAURA ANN STEVENS (daughter of Ronald F Stevens and Alice Jean Marson).

128. **JOE LYNN[6] WHITWORTH** (Imogene F[5] Moore, William Oscar[4] Moore, Daniel Marion[3] Moore, Robert Marian[2] Moore, Zachariah[1] Moore). He married **CAROL DAUGHTERY**.
Joe Lynn Whitworth and Carol Daughtery had the following children:
   i.   DENISE LYNN[7] WHITWORTH (daughter of Joe Lynn Whitworth and Carol Daughtery).
   ii. DONNA MARIE WHITWORTH (daughter of Joe Lynn Whitworth and Carol Daughtery).

129. **PHILLIP DALE[6] WHITWORTH** (Imogene F[5] Moore, William Oscar[4] Moore, Daniel Marion[3] Moore, Robert Marian[2] Moore, Zachariah[1] Moore) was born. He died. He married **VIRGIIA BROOKS**.
Phillip Dale Whitworth and Virgiia Brooks had the following child:
   i.   PHLICIA DIANE[7] BROOKS (daughter of Phillip Dale Whitworth and Virgiia Brooks).

130. **MICHAEL DOUGLASS**[6] **HIPP** (V Maxine[5] Moore, William Oscar[4] Moore, Daniel Marion[3] Moore, Robert Marian[2] Moore, Zachariah[1] Moore). He married **ELLEN AYERS**.
Michael Douglass Hipp and Ellen Ayers had the following child:
   i.   BRYAN DOUGLASS[7] HIPP (son of Michael Douglass Hipp and Ellen Ayers).

131. **PAULETTE**[6] **WHITE** (Lewis Herbon[5] Jr, Vernice C.[4] Moore, Daniel Marion[3] Moore, Robert Marian[2] Moore, Zachariah[1] Moore). She married **HAROLD JOHNSON**.

   Harold Johnson and Paulette White had the following children:
   i.   STEVE[7] JOHNSON (son of Harold Johnson and Paulette White).
   ii. PAGE JOHNSON (daughter of Harold Johnson and Paulette White).

132. **NELIA SUE**[6] **MOORE** (Arnell E[5], Robert Bennett[4] II, Daniel Marion[3], Robert Marian[2], Zachariah[1]). She married **UKN**.

   UKN and Nelia Sue Moore had the following child:
   i.   DEBBIE[7] MOORE (daughter of UKN and Nelia Sue Moore).

133. **HARVEY LEE**[6] **SHELTON** (Attice Lola[5] Harvey, Dona Pearl Donie[4] Adams, Nancy A Elizabeth[3] Moore, Robert Marian[2] Moore, Zachariah[1] Moore). He married **DELORES PULLEN**.
Harvey Lee Shelton and Delores Pullen had the following children:
   i.   BEN[7] SHELTON (son of Harvey Lee Shelton and Delores Pullen).
   ii. BRENT SHELTON (son of Harvey Lee Shelton and Delores Pullen).

134. **JAMES CORDELL**[6] **HARVEY** (Brady Cordell[5], Dona Pearl Donie[4] Adams, Nancy A Elizabeth[3] Moore, Robert Marian[2] Moore, Zachariah[1] Moore). He married **SHIRLEY SOUTHERN**.
James Cordell Harvey and Shirley Southern had the following children:
   i.   JAMES RICHARD[7] HARVEY (son of James Cordell Harvey and Shirley Southern).
   ii. MICHAEL CORDELL HARVEY (son of James Cordell Harvey and Shirley Southern).

135. **JAMES EARL**[6] **ADAMS** (Spud Earl[5], Napoleon Eugene[4], Nancy A Elizabeth[3] Moore, Robert Marian[2] Moore, Zachariah[1] Moore).
James Earl Adams had the following children:
   i.   LOIS[7] ADAMS (daughter of James Earl Adams and).
   ii. KAREN ADAMS (daughter of James Earl Adams and).

136. **JOANN**[6] **ADAMS** (Spud Earl[5], Napoleon Eugene[4], Nancy A Elizabeth[3] Moore, Robert Marian[2] Moore, Zachariah[1] Moore). She married **L.D. CORBELL**.
L.D. Corbell and JoAnn Adams had the following children:
   i.   BRYAN[7] CORBELL (son of L.D. Corbell and JoAnn Adams).
   ii. DONNA JOE CORBELL (daughter of L.D. Corbell and JoAnn Adams).
   iii. CRAIG ALLEN CORBELL (son of L.D. Corbell and JoAnn Adams).

137. **Douglass[6] Steffanauer Jr.** (Lydoth[5] Adams, Napoleon Eugene[4] Adams, Nancy A Elizabeth[3] Moore, Robert Marian[2] Moore, Zachariah[1] Moore). He married **Julie Cunningham**.
Douglass Steffanauer Jr. and Julie Cunningham had the following children:
     i.   **Paul[7] Steffanauer** (son of Douglass Steffanauer Jr. and Julie Cunningham).
     ii. **Ronnie Steffanauer** (son of Douglass Steffanauer Jr. and Julie Cunningham).

138. **Betty Fay[6] Adams** (Gussie Lewis[5], Laborn Elijah[4], Nancy A Elizabeth[3] Moore, Robert Marian[2] Moore, Zachariah[1] Moore). She married **John L. Larue**.
John L. Larue and Betty Fay Adams had the following children:
     i.   **Darlene[7] Larue** (daughter of John L. Larue and Betty Fay Adams).
     ii. **Dowling Ewayne Larue** (son of John L. Larue and Betty Fay Adams).

139. **Gladys[6] Adams** (Gussie Lewis[5], Laborn Elijah[4], Nancy A Elizabeth[3] Moore, Robert Marian[2] Moore, Zachariah[1] Moore). She married **Oliver J. Smith**.
Oliver J. Smith and Gladys Adams had the following children:

   Christopher Lynn[7] Smith (son of Oliver J. Smith and Gladys Adams).
     i.   **Phillip Eugene Smith** (son of Oliver J. Smith and Gladys Adams).
     ii. **Steven Joy Smith** (son of Oliver J. Smith and Gladys Adams).

140. **Fred Jackson[6] Adams** (Gussie Lewis[5], Laborn Elijah[4], Nancy A Elizabeth[3] Moore, Robert Marian[2] Moore, Zachariah[1] Moore) was born on 20 Apr 1937 in Brooksville, Blount, Alabama, United States. He died on 15 Apr 1976 in Arab, Marshall, Alabama, United States of America. He married **Ruth Thompson**.

Fred Jackson Adams and Ruth Thompson had the following children:
     i.   **Danny Lynn[7] Adams** (son of Fred Jackson Adams and Ruth Thompson) was born on 30 Jun 1966. He died on 09 Jul 1982.
     ii. **Michael Edward Adams** (son of Fred Jackson Adams and Ruth Thompson).
     iii. **Annetia Sue Adams** (daughter of Fred Jackson Adams and Ruth Thompson) was born on 29 May 1959. She died on 23 Mar 1987.
     iv. **Sandra E. Adams** (daughter of Fred Jackson Adams and Ruth Thompson).

141. **Maxie Sue[6] Adams** (Gussie Lewis[5], Laborn Elijah[4], Nancy A Elizabeth[3] Moore, Robert Marian[2] Moore, Zachariah[1] Moore). She married **Jack L. Rigsby**.
Jack L. Rigsby and Maxie Sue Adams had the following child:
   181. i. **Brenda[7] Rigsby** (daughter of Jack L. Rigsby and Maxie Sue Adams). She married **Robert Sullivan**.

142. **Donald L.[6] Adams** (Gussie Lewis[5], Laborn Elijah[4], Nancy A Elizabeth[3] Moore, Robert Marian[2] Moore, Zachariah[1] Moore). He married **Verlie M. Laten**.
Donald L. Adams and Verlie M. Laten had the following children:
     i.   **Cathy Dianne[7] Adams** (daughter of Donald L. Adams and Verlie M. Laten).
     ii. **Randall Adams** (son of Donald L. Adams and Verlie M. Laten).

143. **Jimmy**^{6} **Adams** (Aldie^5, Laborn Elijah^4, Nancy A Elizabeth^3 Moore, Robert Marian^2 Moore, Zachariah^1 Moore). He married **Lillian Mnu**.
Jimmy Adams and Lillian MNU had the following children:
     i.   Jim^7 Adams (son of Jimmy Adams and Lillian MNU).
     ii. Julie Adams (daughter of Jimmy Adams and Lillian MNU).

144. **Barbara**^{6} **Adams** (Aldie^5, Laborn Elijah^4, Nancy A Elizabeth^3 Moore, Robert Marian^2 Moore, Zachariah^1 Moore). She married **Clifford Mason**.
Clifford Mason and Barbara Adams had the following children:
     i.   Barry^7 Mason (son of Clifford Mason and Barbara Adams).
     ii. Sherry Mason (daughter of Clifford Mason and Barbara Adams).

145. **Billy**^{6} **Adams** (Aldie^5, Laborn Elijah^4, Nancy A Elizabeth^3 Moore, Robert Marian^2 Moore, Zachariah^1 Moore). He married **Doris Reeves**.
Billy Adams and doris Reeves had the following child:
     i.   Karon^7 Adams (daughter of Billy Adams and doris Reeves).

146. **Hoyt E**^{6} **Adams** (Aldie^5, Laborn Elijah^4, Nancy A Elizabeth^3 Moore, Robert Marian^2 Moore, Zachariah^1 Moore) was born about 1928 in Alabama. He married **Ruby J. Nix**.
Hoyt E Adams and Ruby J. Nix had the following children:
     i.   Jeffery^7 Adams (son of Hoyt E Adams and Ruby J. Nix).
     ii. Steve Adams (son of Hoyt E Adams and Ruby J. Nix).
     iii. Roger Adams (son of Hoyt E Adams and Ruby J. Nix).

147. **Mavis G**^{6} **Adams** (Aldie^5, Laborn Elijah^4, Nancy A Elizabeth^3 Moore, Robert Marian^2 Moore, Zachariah^1 Moore) was born about 1930 in Alabama. She married **Hubert Smith**.
Hubert Smith and Mavis G Adams had the following children:
     i.   Debra Adams^7 Smith (daughter of Hubert Smith and Mavis G Adams). She married Rickey Hamby.
     ii. Donald Adams Smith (son of Hubert Smith and Mavis G Adams).
     iii. Wanda Adams Smith (daughter of Hubert Smith and Mavis G Adams).
     iv. Deanne Adams Smith (daughter of Hubert Smith and Mavis G Adams).

148. **James E**^{6} **Adams** (Ellis^5, Laborn Elijah^4, Nancy A Elizabeth^3 Moore, Robert Marian^2 Moore, Zachariah^1 Moore) was born about 1930 in Alabama. He married **Lillma Yancey**.
James E Adams and Lillma yancey had the following children:
     i.   Dennis^7 Adams (son of James E Adams and Lillma yancey).
183. ii. Wendell Adams (son of James E Adams and Lillma yancey).

149. **MARGARET**[6] **ADAMS** (Ellis[5], Laborn Elijah[4], Nancy A Elizabeth[3] Moore, Robert Marian[2] Moore, Zachariah[1] Moore). She married **BUCK WEBB**.

Buck Webb and Margaret Adams had the following children:

    i.   ROBERT[7] WEBB (son of Buck Webb and Margaret Adams).

    ii.   DEBRA WEBB (daughter of Buck Webb and Margaret Adams).

150. **BOBBIE JEANETTE**[6] **ADAMS** (Ellis[5], Laborn Elijah[4], Nancy A Elizabeth[3] Moore, Robert Marian[2] Moore, Zachariah[1] Moore) was born on 31 Jan 1932 in Alabama. She died on 06 Sep 2001 in Alabama. She married **HERBERT STEVENSON**. He was born on 01 Jul 1925 in Alabama, USA. He died on 13 Jan 1993 in Alabama.

Herbert Stevenson and Bobbie Jeanette Adams had the following children:

    i.   KENNETH[7] STEVENSON (son of Herbert Stevenson and Bobbie Jeanette Adams).

183.   ii.   KARON STEVENSO (daughter of Herbert Stevenson and Bobbie Jeanette Adams). She married **LARRY STONE**.

151. **PATRICIA GAIL**[6] **ADAMS** (Mack[5], Laborn Elijah[4], Nancy A Elizabeth[3] Moore, Robert Marian[2] Moore, Zachariah[1] Moore). She married **JAMES T. WARD**.

James T. Ward and Patricia Gail Adams had the following child:

    i.   DONNA GAIL[7] WARD (daughter of James T. Ward and Patricia Gail Adams).

152. **GAYNELL**[6] **ADAMS** (Mack[5], Laborn Elijah[4], Nancy A Elizabeth[3] Moore, Robert Marian[2] Moore, Zachariah[1] Moore). She married (1) **JERRY WARNICK**. She married (2) **JAMES H. FLACK**.

Jerry Warnick and Gaynell Adams had the following child:

    i.   DONALD JEFFERY[7] WARNICK (son of Jerry Warnick and Gaynell Adams).

153. **JOHNNY MAC**[6] **ADAMS** (Mack[5], Laborn Elijah[4], Nancy A Elizabeth[3] Moore, Robert Marian[2] Moore, Zachariah[1] Moore). He married **BARBARA ATCHLEY**.

Johnny Mac Adams and Barbara Atchley had the following children:

    i.   PHILLIP WAYNE[7] ADAMS (son of Johnny Mac Adams and Barbara Atchley).

    ii.   RHONDA KAY ADAMS (daughter of Johnny Mac Adams and Barbara Atchley).

154. **LUCILLE**[6] **ADAMS** (Mack[5], Laborn Elijah[4], Nancy A Elizabeth[3] Moore, Robert Marian[2] Moore, Zachariah[1] Moore). She married **L. HERRING**.

L. Herring and Lucille Adams had the following children:

    i.   LEWIS C.[7] HERRING (son of L. Herring and Lucille Adams).

    ii.   LARRY JOE HERRING (son of L. Herring and Lucille Adams).

    iii. MICHAEL HERRING (son of L. Herring and Lucille Adams).

155. **EVELYN**[6] **ADAMS** (Mack[5], Laborn Elijah[4], Nancy A Elizabeth[3] Moore, Robert Marian[2] Moore, Zachariah[1] Moore). She married **JACK OSBORN**.

Jack Osborn and Evelyn Adams had the following children:

    i.   HERBERT LEE[7] OSBORN (son of Jack Osborn and Evelyn Adams).

    ii.   TERRY MACK OSBORN (son of Jack Osborn and Evelyn Adams).

    iii. JACKIE OSBORN (son of Jack Osborn and Evelyn Adams).

156. VIRGINIA^6 BESHEARS (Lena^5 Adams, Laborn Elijah^4 Adams, Nancy A Elizabeth^3 Moore, Robert Marian^2 Moore, Zachariah^1 Moore). She married TOM BATES.
Tom Bates and Virginia Beshears had the following child:
  i.   TOMMY^7 BATES JR. (son of Tom Bates and Virginia Beshears).

157. CHARLES^6 BESHEARS (Lena^5 Adams, Laborn Elijah^4 Adams, Nancy A Elizabeth^3 Moore, Robert Marian^2 Moore, Zachariah^1 Moore). He married NONA MURPHREE.
Charles Beshears and Nona Murphree had the following children:
  i.   CHUCKY^7 BESHEARS (son of Charles Beshears and Nona Murphree).
  ii. GREGORY BESHEARS (son of Charles Beshears and Nona Murphree).

158. MAGGIE^6 BESHEARS (Lena^5 Adams, Laborn Elijah^4 Adams, Nancy A Elizabeth^3 Moore, Robert Marian^2 Moore, Zachariah^1 Moore). She married (1) BOBBY PATTERNSON. She married (2) RAY DUPREE.

Bobby Patternson and Maggie Beshears had the following children:
  i.   MARK^7 PATTERNSON (son of Bobby Patternson and Maggie Beshears).
  ii. ROBBIE PATTERNSON (daughter of Bobby Patternson and Maggie Beshears).

Ray Dupree and Maggie Beshears had the following child:
  i.   MICHAEL^7 DUPREE (son of Ray Dupree and Maggie Beshears).

159. SUE^6 BESHEARS (Lena^5 Adams, Laborn Elijah^4 Adams, Nancy A Elizabeth^3 Moore, Robert Marian^2 Moore, Zachariah^1 Moore). She married BILL STEWART.
Bill Stewart and Sue Beshears had the following children:
  i.   LORI^7 STEWART (daughter of Bill Stewart and Sue Beshears).
  ii. STEVE STEWART (son of Bill Stewart and Sue Beshears).
  iii. PAM STEWART (daughter of Bill Stewart and Sue Beshears).

160. RUTH^6 BESHEARS (Lena^5 Adams, Laborn Elijah^4 Adams, Nancy A Elizabeth^3 Moore, Robert Marian^2 Moore, Zachariah^1 Moore). She married JUNIOR SNELL.
Junior Snell and Ruth Beshears had the following children:
  i.   BARRY^7 SNELL (son of Junior Snell and Ruth Beshears).
  ii. DAVID SNELL (son of Junior Snell and Ruth Beshears).
  iii. ERIC SNELL (son of Junior Snell and Ruth Beshears).
  iv. RONNIE SNELL (son of Junior Snell and Ruth Beshears).

161. NADINE^6 BROWN (V Jo^5 Adams, Laborn Elijah^4 Adams, Nancy A Elizabeth^3 Moore, Robert Marian^2 Moore, Zachariah^1 Moore). She married BOBBY LAMB.
Bobby Lamb and Nadine Brown had the following children:
  i.   TIM^7 LAMB (son of Bobby Lamb and Nadine Brown).
  ii. SUSAN LAMB (daughter of Bobby Lamb and Nadine Brown).

162. **JAMES^6 ADAMS** (Rector^5, Laborn Elijah^4, Nancy A Elizabeth^3 Moore, Robert Marian^2 Moore, Zachariah^1 Moore). He married **MARY LARUE**.
James Adams and Mary Larue had the following child:
   i.   TODD^7 ADAMS (son of James Adams and Mary Larue).

163. **KENNETH^6 ADAMS** (Rector^5, Laborn Elijah^4, Nancy A Elizabeth^3 Moore, Robert Marian^2 Moore, Zachariah^1 Moore). He married **GAIL ROSCOE**.
Kenneth Adams and Gail Roscoe had the following child:
   i.   DARRELL^7 ADAMS (son of Kenneth Adams and Gail Roscoe).

164. **COLEMAN^6 TEAGUE** (C Pearl^5 Adams, Laborn Elijah^4 Adams, Nancy A Elizabeth^3 Moore, Robert Marian^2 Moore, Zachariah^1 Moore). He married **BETTY J SNELL**.
Coleman Teague and Betty j Snell had the following child:
   i.   TONY^7 TEAGUE (son of Coleman Teague and Betty j Snell).

165. **FRANCES^6 TEAGUE** (C Pearl^5 Adams, Laborn Elijah^4 Adams, Nancy A Elizabeth^3 Moore, Robert Marian^2 Moore, Zachariah^1 Moore). She married **JAMES BULLARD**.
James Bullard and Frances Teague had the following children:
   i.   STEVE^7 BULLARD (son of James Bullard and Frances Teague).
   ii. RODNEY BULLARD (son of James Bullard and Frances Teague).
   iii. TOMMY BULLARD (son of James Bullard and Frances Teague).

166. **CAROLYN^6 BARNES** (Eulas Flare^5, Sally Emmer Abagel^4 Adams, Nancy A Elizabeth^3 Moore, Robert Marian^2 Moore, Zachariah^1 Moore). She married **WILLIAM THOMPSON**.
William Thompson and Carolyn Barnes had the following children:
   i.   JUDITH CAROL^7 THOMPSON (daughter of William Thompson and Carolyn Barnes).
   ii. DOUGLASS LEE THOMPSON (son of William Thompson and Carolyn Barnes).

167. **S. W.^{6} BESHEARS** (Plumie^5 Barnes, Sally Emmer Abagel^4 Adams, Nancy A Elizabeth^3 Moore, Robert Marian^2 Moore, Zachariah^1 Moore) was born about 1930 in Alabama. He married **HARRIET SOLTER**.
S. W. Beshears and Harriet Solter had the following children:
   i.   GEORGIA^7 BESHEARS (daughter of S. W. Beshears and Harriet Solter).
   ii. REBA BESHEARS (daughter of S. W. Beshears and Harriet Solter).

168. **DOROTHY SUE^6 BESHEARS** (Plumie^5 Barnes, Sally Emmer Abagel^4 Adams, Nancy A Elizabeth^3 Moore, Robert Marian^2 Moore, Zachariah^1 Moore) was born on 24 Jan 1931. She died on 06 Feb 1996 in Gadsden, Etowah, Alabama, United States of America. She married (1) **EASLEY KIRBY**. She married (2) **JIMMY CRUMP**. She married (3) **JOHN P PHILLIPS** on 14 Sep 1963 in Gadsden, Etowah, Alabama, United States of America. He was born on 27 Nov 1918. He died on 23 Apr 2007 in Gadsden, Etowah, Alabama, United States of America.

Jimmy Crump and Dorothy Sue Beshears had the following child:

      i.   BRENDA JEAN^7 CRUMP (daughter of Jimmy Crump and Dorothy Sue Beshears) was born on 16 Nov 1947 in Alabama, USA. She died on 30 Mar 1953 in Etowah, Alabama, USA.

169.   CHARLOTTE ANN^6 BARNES (Oren E^5, Sally Emmer Abagel^4 Adams, Nancy A Elizabeth^3 Moore, Robert Marian^2 Moore, Zachariah^1 Moore). She married FRANK MOOTY.

Frank Mooty and Charlotte Ann Barnes had the following child:

      i.   CYNTHIA^7 MOOTY (daughter of Frank Mooty and Charlotte Ann Barnes).

Generation 7

170.   ANITA ASHLEY^7 MAY (Betty Jo^6 Moore, Edwin Leon^5 Moore, James Robert^4 Moore, Benjamin Martin^3 Moore, Robert Marian^2 Moore, Zachariah^1 Moore) was born on 07 Jul 1953.

Anita Ashley May had the following child:

      i.   BLAKE^8 MAY.

171.   VICKI ASHLEY^7 BAURAIN (Betty Jo^6 Moore, Edwin Leon^5 Moore, James Robert^4 Moore, Benjamin Martin^3 Moore, Robert Marian^2 Moore, Zachariah^1 Moore) was born on 26 Apr 1956.

Vicki Ashley Baurain had the following children:

      i.   CHANEY^8 WELLS was born on 22 May 1993.

      ii.   RANDA BAURAIN was born on 20 Sep 1995.

172.   DANA^7 MOORE (Dan Robert^6, Edwin Leon^5, James Robert^4, Benjamin Martin^3, Robert Marian^2, Zachariah^1) was born in 1957. She married STEVE LANGFORD.

Steve Langford and Dana Moore had the following children:

      i.   MARY ANN^8 LANGFORD (daughter of Steve Langford and Dana Moore).

      ii.   DAGNE LANGFORD (daughter of Steve Langford and Dana Moore).

173.   MIKE^7 MOORE (Dan Robert^6, Edwin Leon^5, James Robert^4, Benjamin Martin^3, Robert Marian^2, Zachariah^1) was born in 1959. He married NOT NAMED.

Mike Moore and not named had the following children:

      i.   GANTT^8 MOORE (son of Mike Moore and not named).

      ii.   DAILEY MOORE (daughter of Mike Moore and not named).

      iii.   CHARLIE MOORE (daughter of Mike Moore and not named).

174.   MATT^7 MOORE (Dan Robert^6, Edwin Leon^5, James Robert^4, Benjamin Martin^3, Robert Marian^2, Zachariah^1) was born in 1962. He married TAMMY SAUNDERS.

Matt Moore and Tammy Saunders had the following children:

      i.   ELIZABETH ANN^8 MOORE (daughter of Matt Moore and Tammy Saunders).

      ii.   AMELIA MOORE (daughter of Matt Moore and Tammy Saunders).

175. **ALAN RUSSELL**[7] **JACKSON** (Constance Marie[6] Currey, Constance Ivaleen[5] Moore, Charles Claude[4] Moore, Dr. James "Jimmy" Hamilton[3] Moore D.MD, Robert Marian[2] Moore, Zachariah[1] Moore) was born on 01 Nov 1966 in Oneonta, Blount, Alabama, USA. He married **TERESA VAN WAGNER**. She was born in Mar 1971.

Alan Russell Jackson and Teresa Van Wagner had the following children:
   i.   TRACY ALANA[8] JACKSON (daughter of Alan Russell Jackson and Teresa Van Wagner) was born on 09 Nov 1991. She married COREY SANDERS.
   ii. KEITH ALAN JACKSON (son of Alan Russell Jackson and Teresa Van Wagner) was born on 07 Sep 1996.

176. **SCOTT CHRISTOPHER**[7] **JACKSON** (Constance Marie[6] Currey, Constance Ivaleen[5] Moore, Charles Claude[4] Moore, Dr. James "Jimmy" Hamilton[3] Moore D.MD, Robert Marian[2] Moore, Zachariah[1] Moore) was born on 01 Feb 1971 in Oneonta, Blount, Alabama, USA. He married (1) **MONICA SUZANNE MYRICK** on 04 Nov 1990 in Snead, Blount, Alabama, USA (Bethel Baptist Church). She was born on 11 Jul 1973. He married (2) **JULIA REBECCA DENISE EVANS** on 01 Sep 2002 in Oneonta, Blount, Alabama, USA. She was born on 19 Apr 1975.
Scott Christopher Jackson and Monica Suzanne Myrick had the following children:
   i.   JESSICA ERIN[8] JACKSON (daughter of Scott Christopher Jackson and Monica Suzanne Myrick) was born on 14 Oct 1992.
   ii. LEVI SCOTT JACKSON (son of Scott Christopher Jackson and Monica Suzanne Myrick) was born on 04 Dec 1996.
Scott Christopher Jackson and Julia Rebecca Denise Evans had the following child:
   iii. EMILY PAIGE ELLIS (daughter of Scott Christopher Jackson and Julia Rebecca Denise Evans) was born on 05 Jun 1993.

177. **JASON ERIC**[7] **JACKSON** (Constance Marie[6] Currey, Constance Ivaleen[5] Moore, Charles Claude[4] Moore, Dr. James "Jimmy" Hamilton[3] Moore D.MD, Robert Marian[2] Moore, Zachariah[1] Moore) was born on 21 Oct 1975 in Etowah, Gadsden, AL US. He married **JAMI ALLYSON WEIR** on 19 Dec 1998 in Gatlinburg, Sevier, Tennessee, USA. She was born on 27 Aug 1977.

Jason Eric Jackson and Jami Allyson Weir had the following child:
   i.   DAVIS MATTHEW[8] JACKSON (son of Jason Eric Jackson and Jami Allyson Weir) was born on 09 Dec 2005 in Arab, Marshall, Alabama, United States.

178. **JOHN KEVIN**[7] **SISSON** (Rebecca Elaine[6] Miller, Leila Rebecca[5] Moore, Charles Claude[4] Moore, Dr. James "Jimmy" Hamilton[3] Moore D.MD, Robert Marian[2] Moore, Zachariah[1] Moore) was born on 26 Jan 1971. He married **JILL GARDNER** on 02 Sep 1994. She was born on 07 Mar 1973.

John Kevin Sisson and Jill Gardner had the following children:
   i.   ASHLEY CHEYENNE[8] SISSON (daughter of John Kevin Sisson and Jill Gardner) was born on 03 Aug 1996.
   ii. MADISON GRACE SISSON (daughter of John Kevin Sisson and Jill Gardner) was born on 19 Feb 2002.

179. **MARK**[7] **RODDAM** (Janet Roberta[6] Oden, Ada Ethel[5] Moore, Charles Claude[4] Moore, Dr. James "Jimmy" Hamilton[3] Moore D.MD, Robert Marian[2] Moore, Zachariah[1] Moore). He married **TAMMY DALE** on 21 Apr 1990.

Mark Roddam and Tammy Dale had the following children:

i. RODDAM[8] MARK JR. (son of Mark Roddam and Tammy Dale) was born on 20 Dec 1990.

ii. SAMANTHA RODDAM (daughter of Mark Roddam and Tammy Dale) was born on 07 May 1996.

180. LISA[7] RODDAM (Janet Roberta[6] Oden, Ada Ethel[5] Moore, Charles Claude[4] Moore, Dr. James "Jimmy" Hamilton[3] Moore D.MD, Robert Marian[2] Moore, Zachariah[1] Moore) was born on 24 May 1978. She married (1) ERIC MANDELL on 21 Nov 1998. She married (2) CHRIS JOHNSON on 10 Jun 2006. He was born on 02 Apr 1971.

Eric Mandell and Lisa Roddam had the following child:

i. NATALIE[8] MANDELL (daughter of Eric Mandell and Lisa Roddam) was born on 15 Sep 2003.

Chris Johnson and Lisa Roddam had the following children:

i. DAVID[8] JOHNSON (son of Chris Johnson and Lisa Roddam) was born on 05 Oct 1989.

ii. COLLIN JOHNSON (son of Chris Johnson and Lisa Roddam) was born on 03 Nov 2008.

181. BRENDA[7] RIGSBY (Maxie Sue[6] Adams, Gussie Lewis[5] Adams, Laborn Elijah[4] Adams, Nancy A Elizabeth[3] Moore, Robert Marian[2] Moore, Zachariah[1] Moore). She married ROBERT SULLIVAN.
Robert Sullivan and BRENDA Rigsby had the following child:

i. KELVIN FRANK[8] SULLIVAN (son of Robert Sullivan and BRENDA Rigsby).

182. WENDELL[7] ADAMS (James E[6], Ellis[5], Laborn Elijah[4], Nancy A Elizabeth[3] Moore, Robert Marian[2] Moore, Zachariah[1] Moore).
Wendell Adams had the following children:

i. CHRIS[8] ADAMS (son of Wendell Adams and).

ii. MIKE ADAMS (son of Wendell Adams and).

183. KARON[7] STEVENSON (Bobbie Jeanette[6] Adams, Ellis[5] Adams, Laborn Elijah[4] Adams, Nancy A Elizabeth[3] Moore, Robert Marian[2] Moore, Zachariah[1] Moore). She married LARRY STONE.
Larry Stone and Karon Stevenson had the following child:

i. LARRY DANIEL[8] STONE (son of Larry Stone and Karon Stevenson).